T0229602

Managing Digital Innovation in Publishing

Reflecting proactively on a growing industry 'dilemma', this book explores how publishing businesses can and do successfully experiment and innovate in digital publishing through collaboration.

Many sectors of publishing are still structured around print production, with digital innovation in the consumer arena generally focused on different book formats, such as e-books and audiobooks, rather than on brand-new types of products. Publishers need to innovate around different sorts of content and digital formats as consumers change their media habits. However, their pricing, business and risk models, and workflows are reflective of a legacy of print publishing; and as print commands so much revenue, publishers do not want to derail their main business as they experiment. Drawing on an analysis of collaboration and network theory and four in-depth qualitative case studies in different sectors, this research suggests that collaboration, particularly engaging with the wider creative sector, is key to the sustainable development of new types of products. It points to the characteristics of a successful digital collaboration and explains how to manage publishing innovation alongside the existing business, through para-organisations. Considering novel approaches to innovation, such as iterative software-style approaches and agile project management, as well as new business models, such as those employed in games development, the author shows how introducing new people – from software developers to competitors – can help instil a collaborative mindset within the organisation and facilitate constructive experimentation.

Managing Digital Innovation in Publishing will be of interest to upper-level students and researchers of (digital) publishing and related creative industries.

Dr Frania Hall is Senior Lecturer and Course Leader for MA Publishing at the London College of Communication (LCC), University of the Arts, London. Based at the School of Media, she teaches undergraduate and postgraduate students of publishing. Prior to this she worked for 20 years in a variety of publishing sectors, most recently as Publisher with Thompson. Her research centres on digital publishing, creative collaboration and entrepreneurial networks as well as zines and participatory community publishing. She is author of *The Business of Digital Publishing*, now in its second edition.

Managing Digital Innovation in Publishing

Collaborations and Para-Organisations for Creative Change

Frania Hall

Routledge
Taylor & Francis Group

LONDON AND NEW YORK

First published 2024
by Routledge
4 Park Square, Milton Park, Abingdon, Oxon OX14 4RN

and by Routledge
605 Third Avenue, New York, NY 10158

Routledge is an imprint of the Taylor & Francis Group, an informa business

© 2024 Frania Hall

The right of Frania Hall to be identified as author of this work has been asserted in accordance with sections 77 and 78 of the Copyright, Designs and Patents Act 1988.

British Library Cataloguing-in-Publication Data
A catalogue record for this book is available from the British Library

Library of Congress Cataloging-in-Publication Data
Names: Hall, Frania, author.
Title: Managing digital innovation in publishing : collaborations and
    para-organisations for creative change / Frania Hall.
Description: 1st edition. | New York, NY : Routledge, 2024. | Includes
    bibliographical references and index.
Identifiers: LCCN 2024000165 (print) | LCCN 2024000166 (ebook) |
    ISBN 9781032456799 (hardback) | ISBN 9781032456782 (paperback) |
    ISBN 9781003378211 (ebook)
Subjects: LCSH: Organizational change. | Publishers and publishing—
    Technological innovations. | Information technology—Management. |
    Electronic publishing. | Creative thinking—Economic aspects—Research. |
    Business networks—Computer network resources.
Classification: LCC HD58.7 .H3385 2024 (print) | LCC HD58.7 (ebook) |
    DDC 658.3—dc23/eng/20240202
LC record available at https://lccn.loc.gov/2024000165
LC ebook record available at https://lccn.loc.gov/2024000166

ISBN: 978-1-032-45679-9 (hbk)
ISBN: 978-1-032-45678-2 (pbk)
ISBN: 978-1-003-37821-1 (ebk)

DOI: 10.4324/9781003378211

Typeset in Times New Roman
by Apex CoVantage, LLC

In memory of Alan Jarvis, a dear friend.

Contents

1 Introduction

Digital innovation and publishing research

Introduction

Despite the impact of the digital age, publishers have faced challenges when undertaking digital innovation. Several sectors of publishing remain mostly structured around print production; digital innovation in the consumer arena, for example, has generally settled on transferring text directly into ebooks and audio, essentially retaining the basic recognisable format of a book even in digital formats. While journals publishers are in many cases wholly digital, the legacy of the print world is still apparent in their digital form (for example, around volume numbers). Publishers need to innovate continuously with digital formats as consumers change their media habits, but they have found it difficult to experiment in more unexpected directions; there are exciting and acclaimed projects that have fallen by the way. Its pricing, business and risk models, and workflows are reflective of a legacy of print publishing; and as print commands so much revenue, publishers do not want to derail their main business as they experiment.

This book explores how existing publishing businesses successfully experiment and innovate in digital publishing through collaboration. Publishing is collaborating more widely and particularly engaging with the wider creative sector; it recognises this is an important way to develop new types of products. Through an analysis of collaboration and network theory, through aligning publishing with the wider creative sector and through four in-depth qualitative case studies in different publishing sectors, this research outlines:

1) the characteristics of a successful digital collaboration for publishing,
2) how to manage publishing innovation alongside the existing business, through para-organisations,
3) how a developing a collaborative mindset within the organisation is important to be able to achieve this.

DOI: 10.4324/9781003378211-1

Scope: publishing sectors

While publishing can be discussed in a general sense, there are clearly differences between the ways different sectors operate. As an example, the specialist sectors will more proactively commission titles, building on market research; this market has specific requirements, well understood by publishers, and the market also has clear expectations, understands the value of the content when they use it and has direct relationships with publishers (Thompson, 2005). The trade sector will more often acquire books via literary agents and will spend more money on marketing titles creatively in order to draw in an interested market and set up a title as a potential best seller, catching a trend (Thompson, 2012).

Structurally, however, both specialist and trade sectors are set up with a similar range of departments (editorial, production, marketing, etc.) even where, for example, large databases are being developed and managed. Where collaboration takes place, it may be about a specific product or a wider service for a market depending on the sector; but the process of the collaboration is expected to have recognisable characteristics across any sector (or indeed, any industry), and those characteristics are the focus of the study.

The digital shift is playing out across all sectors: while for each sector the way it is changing will be different, and with some necessarily moving more quickly than others towards digital transformation, the fact that it is changing and leading to new collaborations can be seen across all publishing sectors. The research will test whether each sector views collaboration as critical to its operating effectively in a changing environment; it will examine examples from each sector, and it will also see how far these different sectors feel the need to change structures in order to operate effectively.

Publishing as a content industry

In considering how to accommodate the differences between sectors for this research, it may be useful to acknowledge the changing terminologies used in publishing. While once 'book' or 'journal' might be the term used to typify the publishing products of the industry, 'content' is now more frequently referred to (Bhaskar, 2013) and as such covers a range of different content types that can be structured in different ways depending on the market. It is partly the development of digital technologies that has led to this change in terminology – content in digital form becomes fluid in terms of format, and content management systems become frameworks for managing, shaping and distributing content effectively (Bhaskar, 2013).

This view is also driven by those researching creative industries more widely with 'content industries' seen to represent any industry that creates products where the value is the content itself, whether artworks, film, music or written text (Simon and Bogdanowicz, 2012). It can, when one uses 'content'

as the collective term, become easier to discuss concepts that are related to the industry as a whole; concepts such as aggregation and curation, scarcity and abundance can apply to all sorts of content (Shatzkin, 2009). Additionally, commentators talk about the business of publishing being about the business of 'reading' (Lloyd, 2008) or storytelling (Rankin, 2013). 'Content' therefore crosses sectors and types of material effectively, even if it can sound somewhat sterile as a term. This then helps the exploration of publishing theory which can encompass all publishing sectors.

Research methodology

The primary research question centred on exploring creative collaborations in the publishing sector that lead to innovative digital products. This took two angles: the first on the collaboration itself, the second on the context for collaboration within a publishing business. The research first aimed to identify what makes an effective collaboration and explore the characteristics that reflect any new processes and patterns adopted by these collaborations. These are termed *creative collaboration* and are those centred on product development approaches that are unusual or stand out in some way, doing something different and innovative with content. For the second aspect, the same collaborations were also examined in relation to the way they worked alongside the businesses from which they emerged and how this relationship was managed. There was also an exploration of collaborative culture within organisations to examine how easy it would be to set up further collaborative activity. From these two angles, then, the research aimed to draw conclusions about the structural aspects of collaboration as well as what it takes for a collaboration to be successful: this therefore also has a relevance to collaboration theory in that it looks at contextualising collaborative activity and contributes to network theory in the way value is vested in networks for their potentiality to further collaboration.

The methodology for the research follows a postpositivist framework (Alvesson and Skoldberg, 2009; Creswell, 2007, 2014; Davies, 2007; Flick, 2008). The research design is centred on qualitative research, following abductive principles (Alvesson and Skoldberg, 2009; Davies, 2007): Blaikie says, when designing social research, an abductive approach encourages a situation where 'data and theoretical ideas are played off against one other, in a developmental and creative process' (2009:156), reflecting a more iterative process to qualitative research; it also accommodates a level of reflexivity on the part of the researcher who is also an actor within this arena (Alvesson and Skoldberg, 2009; Latour, 2007).

Qualitative research is beneficial for a variety of reasons: primarily it allows for probing into detail, in order to understand why something is going on (Creswell, 2007; Flick, 2008; Huberman and Miles, 2002; Maxwell, 1992). It is in this way that qualitative approaches are able to manage the

'pluralization of life worlds' (Flick, 2008) both at the level of the individual (and their understanding of their collaborative activity), and at the level of the collaboration as a whole (involving many individuals with different approaches to the same activity). Qualitative research also recognises the importance of context (Creswell, 2007) while being appropriate for exploring something temporary, both in terms of the individual experience and in terms of the whole collaboration (Flick, 2008).

The case study approach

A case study approach was adopted, and Yin (2013) was used to frame the research design. As Meyer states, citing Hartley (1994), case studies are often used for organisational research 'where new processes or behaviours are little understood' (Meyer, 2001:330); Yin concurs (2013:39), and Kung states that case studies help build an 'understanding [of] organisations from the perspective of those working in them, with a focus on how meaning is constructed out of events and phenomena' (2016:122). Essentially case studies are useful as they can explore a contemporary phenomenon in depth, can cope with complexity, can take a realist approach and can accommodate 'multiple-realities having multiple meanings' (Yin, 2013:17).

The cases chosen are a purposeful sample, not least because there were not very many examples of creative digital collaboration to select from (Meyer, 2001). This was not regarded necessarily as a limitation, as there were enough to ensure a carefully planned sample. Central to this was being able to choose collaborations from different sectors of the publishing industry to ensure representativeness of different digital product development approaches. Each case contained a variety of different participants, allowing for a rounded view of the collaboration through data collection. The criteria for identifying cases were as follows:

1) Newness – in some way the cases needed to reflect something new, whether in terms of new approach to content or engaging with new partners or new structures; the sample did not include, for example, large database projects which have been well established for some time (such as Westlaw or academic journal databases).
2) A range of different partners which reflected different backgrounds was a requirement.
3) The participants were closely linked to the project while it was being set up: this was in order to examine the creative/visionary/management aspects of the project (which would also inform the structural issues examined later); as such it meant that people who may have worked on the project in more functional roles, such as teams of coders or copy editors, were not explicitly questioned as they would not have much overview on the project.

4) They also had to be enduring in some way (some digital collaborations have been very quick to take place and finish, either purposefully or by accident, and the product now no longer exists, making research into these more complex in terms of varying the data types collecting).

The sample was chosen 'according to the intensity with which the interesting features, processes and experiences and so on are given or assumed in them' (Flick, 2008:122). Four cases were selected and are summarised in the next section.

Data collection

Following Yin's four principles of data collection, the first aspect of case study research is to ensure that more than one data collection method is used. Multiple sources of evidence are critical to ensuring an approach to cases which is not one-sided but adds to the depth of understanding. This helps avoid bias as well as reinforcing the theory and concepts that emerge from it with stronger substantiation (Meyer, 2001). Some research theorists feel that varied data collection methods lack purity, but in Yin's view it adds to the quality of the research (2013:119). If different sorts of evidence converge (2013), then the research findings can be considered more valid; data triangulation of this sort adds depth.

The primary data collection method for each case was semi-structured interviews with a number of participants from each case study. For Latour (2007) interviewing actors and letting them speak for themselves and make their own interpretation of the events in which they participated is central to getting good data. Getting as close as possible to the phenomenon and following the actors through their experience of it (via their narrative) is important to allow the sense-making process to take place within the hands of the actors themselves. The sample of participants from the cases was also carefully planned to ensure a rounded set of interviews. The aim was to ensure that participants came from different parts of the collaboration and from different organisations. For example, one case talked to people in the publishing company, freelancers for the publishing company, people in the arts organisation and freelancers for the arts organisation.

It was also important to triangulate the participants' thinking about the collaboration in order to identify how it operated and to what experiences it led. It was interesting, for instance, to note whether assessments of success were mirrored by all participants. It was not possible to talk to everyone involved in each collaboration, but even for cases that were smaller, it was important that the participants came from different organisations to ensure a contrast could still be drawn.

Care was taken over questionnaire design, following a structure established through the reading that reflected the process of a collaboration: formation,

operation and outcome. Aligned to these three stages were indicators of effective collaborative actions, drawn from collaboration theory, and considered characteristics of networks and cooperation from network theory: indicators included autonomy, sites of power, vision, project management style and identified different roles such as the broker. Collaboration outcomes were also considered – to test how different participants valued the collaboration and what results they expected from it: here it was apparent from the literature that for these sorts of creative collaborations, organisational learning is as important as commercial success.

Interviews were then transcribed, and analysed according to a thematic coding approach using a coding manual (Flick, 2008). In one case where the focus was on collaborative cultures, a larger number of interviews was conducted and NVivo used for the coding stage. A set of coding trees were developed for each of the collaborative stages, aligned to the questionnaire.

Interviews were triangulated with other forms of data collection. Document analysis centred on marketing and press announcements about the collaboration and the projects. Protocols for collection of the corpus and the analysis of the content were put in place. The process of examining data using document analysis was informed by Rapley (2008), Flick (2008), Krippendorf (2004) and Rose (2016). There was also observation of behaviours around collaborative meeting spaces. Two non-participant observations were undertaken, planned and executed with ethical considerations in place. These brought more evidence to bear on interpersonal behaviour of individuals participating in collaborative working (Yin, 2013). The observations followed procedures laid down by Creswell (2007) and Angrosino (2007).

Analysis and Creativity

Having a defined analytical approach is central to being able to ensure findings are robust and valid as well as sound in terms of theory development (Creswell, 2007; Eisenhardt, 1989; Flick, 2008; Rapley, 2008; Yin, 2013). This research has been influenced by Creswell's analysis spiral which reflects the ongoing refinement and interlocking of the processes as the cases are worked for details (2007). Once the case descriptions were established, focus then moved onto explanation-building and pattern-matching in making a cross-case synthesis. The cases were developed individually: first through stages of filtering and selecting in order to understand the operation of a case as an individual entity, recognising its particular characteristics given its context; then they were compared with each other to identify similarities and differences.

As the cases were drawn together, it is important to note how far creativity plays a part in the analysis. For Eisenhardt creativity is important as 'creative insight often arises from the juxtaposition of contradictory or paradoxical evidence' (1989:29); Alvesson and Skoldberg talk of 'intellectual flexibility,

receptiveness and creativity' (2009:305). This, they argue, can lead to a richness well-appointed for qualitative research. Seale (2002) says that imposing methodological standards are necessary, but only 'if it is done in a relatively open and permissive way, that preserves the enterprise of qualitative research as a creative and exploratory enterprise' (2002:108). All this leads to analysis that is thoughtful and valid.

Limitations

There are several limitations to the data – the number of cases and the number of participants, for example – but by following selection procedures it is hoped the research has managed to find a good variety of cases and interviewees. Bias with the participants was possible, depending on whether they viewed the collaboration as successful or not. Nevertheless, the case study approach was designed to accommodate individual viewpoints, and this further reinforced the requirement to undertake the analysis strategy with care when interpreting data.

Some themes emerged at a stage where it was too late to revisit extensively. For instance, some participants discussed the way digital projects come together from a much more technical standpoint; this did appear to elicit interesting data on the different approaches of publishers and digital developers but that emerged late on and was, in any case, beyond the scope of this research.

The products were not chosen based on whether or not they were successful. Participants were asked to suggest what they believed were measures of success and also asked whether they believed the measures were met. However, it has become apparent that the cases were all successful to some extent because they are all still products that are available. Not all digital products survive. There have been notable product closures (e.g. Black Crown from Random House). While it would have been useful to consider collaboration for those that failed in order to compare them with those that succeeded, it was difficult to predict ahead the progress of the products in order to choose a suitable mixture of successes and failures. The findings could be interpreted as successful ways to conduct a collaboration in order to develop a successful product, but that would be inconclusive without comparison to collaborations that may have led to a failed product. The research throughout, however, was more focused on the participants views of successful collaboration, and their measures of success were as often about the collaboration itself and the quality of the product as on the success of the product in the marketplace.

Mini case study methodology

At the end of Chapter 2 there is a mini-case study around industry responses to digital change. This is based on a combined quantitative and qualitative

survey with business leaders. It was intended not to develop theory but to understand the context in which further research could be conducted and bring more granularity to the nature of change as perceived by those within the industry.

Studying those actors within the industry and their own understanding of their position draws something from Bruno Latour (2007) as well as more reflective research methodologies that seek to allow participants' voice (Alvesson and Skoldberg, 2009)

The survey focuses on digital transformation and industry responses. The strategic implications of change and the effect of the emerging themes on organisational behaviour and on new activities are of particular interest. The questions aimed to test the nature of change in terms of how it is perceived by those in the business, examining what most concerns industry leaders and exploring the actions, including collaborative activity, they are undertaking in response to digital transformation.

A non-randomised sample was necessary to ensure the survey reached the appropriate people. Participants needed to have been in the industry for a while in order to be in a position to have experienced a broadly pre-digital environment so they would notice and consider issues of transformation. They also needed to be in senior positions because of the nature of the strategic overview they have, and it was important to have the different sectors and different sizes of company represented. The survey had responses from managing directors and digital directors. Results were thematically coded, with in vivo codes also informing the coding of the main part of the research in relation to collaboration.

Outline of the book

Having introduced the scope and methodology of the book, Chapters 2 and 3 focus on presenting the publishing context. Chapter 2 lays out the way the structure of the industry has evolved in such a way that it potentially limits certain types of innovation. This chapter relates publishing to management and organisational theory, exploring the way publishing mimics many traditional companies in relation to the structure around workflow and the value chain (Bhaskar and Phillips, 2019; Murray and Squires, 2013; Thompson, 2005, 2012, 2021). It outlines the particular features of publishing and the way it currently manages innovation and risk, exploring aspects such as managed oversupply and showing how print and legacy business models can hinder innovation. In considering the way digital publishing has emerged (e.g. around digital production, for example) the chapter explores the challenges in particular around digital product development (Thompson, 2005, 2012). It examines theories around publishing ecosystems and the disrupted value chain as well as the wider environment of changing consumer behaviour in light of technology (Bhaskar, 2013; Murray and Squires, 2013; Scolari, 2019;

Simon and de Prato, 2012). From this we can see that publishing is in one sense limited by its structure – it does not have effective ways to experiment with new digital forms, so it needs to work out how to do so without distorting its business of print and print-derived digital production. The chapter also touches on the mini case study mentioned, which explores how publishing business leaders have been thinking about innovation, and which indicates how central collaboration is to their strategic development. This chapter therefore centres on presenting the case for an adaptation of the structure.

Chapter 3 reviews characteristics of the creative industries sector with reference to publishing – for example, project-based working and attitudes to risk (Hesmondhalgh and Baker, 2011; Hirsch, 1972) – to examine processes' creativity and innovation. It looks at aspects of creative management including flexible working, management around newness, creative teams and managing the process of creativity, showing how they apply to publishing; creative project management styles are explored too, as this looks at ways to manage innovation (Bilton, 2006; Kung, 2016). This review is particularly centred on the fact that publishing is starting to collaborate with a wider range of creative partners and shows how this sector is organised to collaborate.

Having explored how publishing is set up for innovation and considered the creative sectors in which it sits, the next two chapters lay out theoretical frameworks that will be applied in the research: the two interrelated areas are collaboration and networks. Collaboration theory is still to some extent emergent, although there is a lot written about collaboration, whether in relation to theoretical definitions or to observations about practical operation. Chapter 4 explores the aspects of collaboration that in particular apply to creative activity. Through exploring key characteristics of collaboration theory, a series of requirements for effective collaborations emerges: qualities such as convergent and divergent thinking, group formation, vision development, trust and operation and exploratory and experimental strategic collaboration are all central to effective creative collaboration (Kaats and Opheij, 2014; Levine and Moreland, 2004; Sawyer, 2017). This provides tests for the effectiveness of creative collaboration in the publishing sector and outlines the theories to be explored in the case studies.

Successful innovation is driven by new ideas and new approaches: collaboration helps bring new ideas to fruition but how do people make the connections in the first place? Chapter 5 explores network theory in relation to collaborative creative projects, drawing together key theories around strong and weak ties, structural holes, project ecologies, value in networks and entrepreneurial networks (Burt, 2004; Granovetter, 1973; Scolari, 2019); there is reference to the particular roles in networks of the broker who has importance in stimulating collaborative activity. Networks are not only about setting up the collaboration in the first place; they play a part both in the ongoing operation of specific collaborations and also in their being embedded in the ongoing operation of a business as a whole. This chapter applies network behaviour to the publishing industry, building on Heebels et al. (2013) to see how networks are central to effective collaborative working for publishers.

Chapters 6 and 7 present the case studies, looking first at how collaborations work within themselves and then in relation to actions that impact the wider organisation.

Chapter 6 presents successful collaborations from the three different digital projects chosen for the research. The three cases are summarised as follows:

Case 1 is an example of a consumer-oriented game book. A variety of different people from the wider creative sector were involved, from game developers to storyboard artists alongside the publisher which in itself reflected network behaviour. The publisher's involvement in supporting the idea financially reflected a change in approach and the project was also highly experimental.

Case 2 was centred on developing an interactive educational textbook. A publisher and an arts organisation were the primary partners but with a variety of different freelancers taking key roles in the development stages. The overall collaborative relationship was developed for the longer term, and it was particularly important for highlighting the centrality of the broker role.

Case 3 draws out the key issues of a larger academic digital project. Key themes that emerge centre on maintaining a nimble and creative approach to development while managing a complex project which required some formal management processes. The project was also interesting in that it involved collaborating with competitors.

Chapter 6 focuses on examining how these projects are formed, how they operate once in action (particularly in relation to the companies that they come from) and what outcomes they aim for. This draw out themes like vision development and autonomy as well as risk and creativity, and links to the collaborative theories from the previous chapters.

Chapter 7 then draws back to assess the issues that impact the parent organisations. It presents the findings from the three project cases, focusing more on networks and structural issues, looking at the cases more holistically and paying attention to strategies for sustaining digital projects in the longer term. It also includes a fourth case which outlines aspects of a change programme that aimed to instil a collaborative mindset. It looks more closely at internal structures, exploring ways an organisation has created a collaborative culture, one that sets up conditions for effective collaborations and innovation in the future.

The final chapter draws the research and the proposition to a conclusion. It summarises the characteristics of successful digital collaborations as centred on:

• Networks
• Brokers

- Vision
- Range of diverse partners
- Autonomy and trust
- Project management styles and project ecologies
- Types of outcomes with particular focus on organisational learning and creativity

These characteristics will be explained. From this it recognises that to achieve these aspects, a collaboration needs to operate as a small organisation of its own – a para-organisation – that can sit outside the main activity of the organisation but draw on expertise and support as needed. In this sense it outlines a way to integrate and manage digital publishing projects. Each of the three project case studies reflects this essential organisation – which allows for people to take risks, experiment and collaborate in an agile way, even with competitors in some cases. The final case study then shows how a pipeline of potential projects could be developed in the future by establishing an outward-looking collaborative mindset through the company and a culture that enables new ideas to be heard and serendipitous opportunities to occur, thus developing new entrepreneurial networks. This approach to digital publishing, as illustrated by the cases, reflects a way to maintain the current successful business models of publishing while exploring new ones.

References

Alvesson, M., Skoldberg, K., (2009) *Reflexive methodology: New vistas for qualitative research*, 2nd Edn. London: Sage.
Angrosino, M., (2007) *Doing ethnographic and observational research*. London: Sage.
Bhaskar, M., (2013) *The content machine: Towards a theory of publishing from the printing press to the digital network*. London: Anthem Press.
Bhaskar, M., Phillips, A., (2019) The future of publishing: Eight thought experiments, in: *The oxford handbook of publishing*. Oxford: Oxford University Press.
Bilton, C., (2006) *Management and creativity: From creative industries to creative management*. Chichester: John Wiley & Sons.
Blaikie, N., (2009) *Designing social research*, 2nd Edn. Cambridge: Polity.
Burt, R.S., (2004) Structural holes and good ideas. *American Journal of Sociology* 110, 349–399. https://doi.org/10.1086/421787
Creswell, J.W., (2007) *Qualitative inquiry and research design: Choosing among five approaches*, 2nd Edn. Thousand Oaks, CA: Sage.
Creswell, J.W., (2014) *Research design: Qualitative, quantitative, and mixed methods approaches*. Thousand Oaks, CA: Sage.
Davies, M.B., (2007) *Doing a successful research project: Using qualitative or quantitative methods*. Basingstoke: Palgrave Macmillan.
Eisenhardt, K.M., (1989) Building theories from case study research. *The Academy of Management Review* 14, 532–550. https://doi.org/10.2307/258557
Flick, U., (2008) *Designing qualitative research*. London: Sage.
Granovetter, M.S., (1973) The strength of weak ties. *American Journal of Sociology* 78, 1360–1380.

Hartley, J. (1994). Case Studies in Organisational Research in Casell, C., Symon, G., (eds) *Qualitative Methods in Organisational Research*, London: Sage.

Heebels, B., Oedzge, A., van Aalst, I., (2013) Social networks and cultural mediators: The multiplexity of personal ties in publishing. *Industry and Innovation* 20. https://doi.org/10.1080/13662716.2013.856621

Hesmondhalgh, D., Baker, S., (2011) *Creative labour: Media work in three cultural industries*. London: Routledge.

Hirsch, P.M., (1972) Processing fads and fashions: An organization-set analysis of cultural industry systems. *American Journal of Sociology* 77, 639–659.

Huberman, A.M., Miles, M.B., (2002) *The qualitative researcher's companion: classic and contemporary readings*. Thousand Oaks, CA: Sage.

Kaats, E., Opheij, W., (2014) *Creating conditions for promising collaboration: Alliances, networks, chains, strategic partnerships*. New York: Springer.

Krippendorff, K., (2004) *Content analysis: An introduction to its methodology*. London: Sage.

Kung, L., (2016) *Strategic management in the media: Theory to practice*, 2nd Edn. London: Sage.

Latour, B., (2007) *Reassembling the social: An introduction to actor-network-theory*, New Edn. New York: Oxford University Press.

Levine, J.M., Moreland, R.L., (2004) Collaboration: The social context of theory development. *Personality and Social Psychology Review* 8, 164–172. https://doi.org/10.1207/s15327957pspr0802_10

Lloyd, S., (2008) *A book publisher's manifesto for the 21st century*. The Digitalist. http://thedigitalist.net/ (accessed 10.20.12).

Maxwell, J., (1992) Understanding and validity in qualitative research. *Harvard Educational Review* 62, 279–301. https://doi.org/10.17763/haer.62.3.8323320856251826

Meyer, C.B., (2001) A case in case study methodology. *Field Methods* 13, 329–352. https://doi.org/10.1177/1525822X0101300402

Murray, P.R., Squires, C., (2013) The digital publishing communications circuit. *Book 2.0* 3, 3–23. https://doi.org/10.1386/btwo.3.1.3_1

Rankin, J., (2013) HarperCollins UK boss tells publishers: Take storytelling back from digital rivals. *The Guardian*.

Rapley, T., (2008) *Doing conversation, discourse and document analysis*. London: Sage.

Rose, G., (2016) *Visual methodologies: An introduction to researching with visual materials*. London: Sage.

Sawyer, K., (2017) *Group genius: The creative power of collaboration*. London: Hachette.

Scolari, C., (2019) Networks, in: *The Oxford handbook of publishing*. Oxford: Oxford University Press, pp. 127–146.

Seale, C., (2002) Quality issues in qualitative inquiry. *Qualitative Social Work* 1, 97–110. https://doi.org/10.1177/147332500200100107

Shatzkin, M., (2009) *Aggregation and curation: Two concepts that explain a lot about digital change*. The Shatzkin Files. www.idealog.com/blog/

aggregation-and-curation-two-concepts-that-explain-a-lot-about-digital-change/ (accessed 8.15.16).

Simon, J.P., Bogdanowicz, M., (2012) *The digital shift in the media and content industries: Policy brief (policy document no. 1/2013)*. Luxembourg: EUR Scientific and Research Series. European Commission, Joint Research Centre.

Thompson, J.B., (2005) *Books in the digital age: The transformation of academic higher education publishing in Britain and the United States*. Cambridge: Polity.

Thompson, J.B., (2012) *Merchants of culture: The publishing business in the twenty-first century*. Cambridge: Polity Press.

Thompson, J.B., (2021) *Book wars: The digital revolution in publishing*. Chichester: John Wiley & Sons

Yin, R.K., (2013) *Case study research: Design and methods*, 5th Edn. Los Angeles, CA: Sage.

2 The structure of publishing organisations

Introduction

The business structures and working systems in publishing have developed over a long period, centred on the production of books and journals. These products have moved successfully into digital environments, particularly in terms of production processes and distribution. Publishing innovation in the recent past has focused on finding and developing new content and on refining production processes and workflows; it has focused less on developing new formats particularly in the digital sphere. eBooks are new digital formats in one sense, but they essentially mimic the form of a book; online journals are sophisticated digital products, but at the heart the article is still similar to a print article. The case studies presented in this book focus on creative digital collaborations which are experimenting with using the digital formats in different ways; a more innovative digital product sits at the heart of these projects – whether an interactive multimedia educational resource or a gamified storytelling device.

One of the aspects being explored by the research is whether these sorts of collaborations reflect a different way of working that does not fit within existing business structures. The traditional structure of the publishing house is in many ways rigid, counter to innovative practices. This chapter therefore outlines the way the businesses structures have evolved over recent decades, with particular focus on workflows; it examines the way digital publishing has emerged within these frameworks in order to ask how far the structures might impede certain types of innovation, therefore requiring new modes of collaborative working.

Structure of a traditional publishing business

The current structures within the publishing industry tend to reflect the organisation of a traditional production-based business, set up around departments that take on different functions for this production (Baverstock et al., 2015; Darnton, 2010; Hall, 2019; Hirsch, 1972; Ray Murray and Squires, 2013). It is most usually organised around function: commissioning or acquisitions,

DOI: 10.4324/9781003378211-2

desk editorial, production and design, distribution, marketing and professional services like finance. There are variations around these departments, as some roles are freelanced out or centralised across different imprints, for example. However, the organisation chart for a generic publishing business would be reasonably recognisable across the industry, and as such reflects what might be regarded as 'traditional publishing'. While many industries will have research and development departments (R&D) or product design departments, the commissioning or acquisitions part of editorial is the revenue driver for the publishing business, developing new products by seeking out talented authors and signing up new content.

These departments will cooperate in the development of an individual book or list, but also will tend to have their own imperatives to follow around cost management or sales targets. These functions mimic the traditional workflow of a publishing business: each stage in the process for the production of a book is overseen by a different department: the book passes through each stage of this production line from editorial to sales and marketing.

The organisation of any business around specific roles reflects the management thinking of the twentieth century; each part of the structure has highly developed expertise, and participants refine and hone the part of the process for which they are responsible. This structure has for many years allowed for smooth working of publishing operations: publishers take risks in terms of deciding which new content they feel will be successful, which they put into the workflow. Once commissioned, all other aspects of the system work in highly developed ways to ensure the smooth production of that content in published form.

If publishing and commissioning editors are seen to be the research and development part of the business, it is possible they need to focus further on new formats as part of this role. What in a sense is missing is a clear approach to digital experimentation, and publishing houses have done this in different ways, maybe with a digital department or adding digital commissioning onto the work of the editor. New digital formats can be complex to develop. Publishing houses of course do develop digital products, and large organisations such as law publishers have adopted approaches that are more akin to iterative software development for the storing and management of content, and for the output of that content. Nevertheless, for many publishers the traditional management processes of the twentieth century are not suited to experimentation and risk taking, in particular accommodating the possibility of failing as much as the requirement to succeed.

The structure of the value chain and its limitations

The concept of the value chain is a well-established framework for understanding business activity and is a key element in understanding both the processes of publishing and the current structure it has adopted. This framework often dominates concepts of publishing, describing as it does the essential functions of the publishing process in organisational and management terms. Though, by focusing on a business approach, it does not necessarily reach into the more fundamental aspects of what publishing is and what it does for us as a society.

The value chain, emerging from Porter's theory about competitive advantage (1985) as applied to publishing, outlines the stages in the progress of a book from author to reader. At each stage the publisher adds something to the end product (Hall, 2019; Thompson, 2012); for example, it may be the textual work that refines the writing, the design of pages to maximise on clarity of the content, marketing focus to attract and reach markets or author branding to increase awareness of backlists (Thompson, 2012). As a standard production line, the process is in many ways linear, and, although some activities will happen concurrently, the process has a beginning (the raw content), and an end (the final output) – directed to the market via intermediaries with whom the publishers have well-established links. In general, the individual components of the value chain reflect the various functions involved.

One particular aspect of this is the importance of protecting the value chain. By framing the input into the chain as intellectual property, in many ways, it intensifies what it is the publisher has hold of at the start of the process. By adding value at each stage, the publisher is protecting the intellectual property (of theirs or of the authors), making it 'more' unique, more usable and more accessible (through anything from design or distribution); the notion of protection is perhaps more of an issue in a digital age in which trying to protect content becomes a challenge (whether from piracy, from re-mixing, etc.). With the ethos of an internet that allows for sharing and exchange along the principle of open access, this overt protection of intellectual property can be controversial (Naughton, 2012).

The value chain is adapting and being broken down in various ways by digital change (Ray Murray and Squires, 2013; Steiner, 2018; Thompson, 2012). Not all elements of the value chain are required; digital books do not need brick-and-mortar bookshops, for instance. Many outputs are possible with digital formats, and the start and end points of a project are less clear as content can be under continuous development (for instance, real-time updating of legal products or online, open access, peer-review systems mean continuous writing is going on).

Quality and the nature of value become more nuanced when considered in light of a more democratised publishing environment with the onset of digital production and products. For example, the activities of the sales and marketing functions are focused not just on promoting and selling products but on finding new consumers and building new audience relationships (Thompson, 2012). Nevertheless, while the nature of the value changes, that each stage adds something is still central.

The communications circuit also takes a functional and process approach to the structure of a publishing business. Darnton develops this theoretical approach (2002, 2010) as a way to look for the fundamental elements of book production from author to publisher and via bookseller to reader. There are elements in common with the value chain, though it takes a wider view by including the reader, for example; and Darnton uses this as a way to tie different disciplinary approaches together (including literary theory and book history). It is interesting to consider this also in light of digital developments; as Ray Murray and Squires (2013) reflect, the communications circuit is adaptable. It too reflects a process that focuses essentially on production and distribution and less on new product development. These concepts offer flexible ways to identify different functions within publishing and understand how to improve on them with technology. New ways for works to be published, made possible by digital technology such as through self-publishing websites, crowdfunded works or open access models, can also be regarded as aspects of the value chain or communications circuit.

Concepts of risk and new product development in publishing

The publishing industry is a creative one, and new product development is naturally central to its processes. However, the way new product development has traditionally tended to manifest itself is in a particular set of commissioning and acquisition processes. By signing up new titles, some of which will be more successful than others, there is an understanding of taking risks; but it can be argued that this approach to risk is very much controlled by certain established rules played out in the field, which differs from processes for digital experimentation and innovation (Coser, 1975; Hirsch, 1972).

For instance, overproduction of titles can be regarded as a way of managing the risk: it is expected that only some titles will make it through to become best sellers out of all those that are signed up, and so an expectation of failure is built into the system. The pareto rule (Jenkins, 2006; Thompson, 2012) applied to publishing would indicate that publishers make the 80% of revenues from 20% of books; this leads to the requirement to produce a certain number of books in order for there to be best sellers. Hirsch summarises 'under these conditions it apparently is more efficient to produce many "failures" for each success than sponsor fewer items' (1972:504). Meanwhile, Coser (1975) considers that getting the balance between commercial stability and product experimentation has led to certain practices centred on managing risk (overproduction) and developing network behaviours (to identify new talent). He states,

> in an industry faced with a high degree of market insecurity and unpredictability, and where capital investment for each book is relatively low, it appears a rational organisational response to follow a shotgun principle, scattering many shots in the hope that at least a few hit the targets.
>
> (1975:21)

This approach to new product risk is in fact more bureaucratic; it is embedded in the behaviour and workflow of the organisation as well as the commercial structures of the profit and loss account. Negus points to the fact that the systems used to manage cultural production in creative industries are embedded: 'symbolic material is constructed as a result of very well-established routines that require little effort or sourcing' (2002:510). Systems that are entrenched, while they run very smoothly, may not be equipped to deal with change effectively. Working practices that are institutionalised can cause problems and allow for little flexibility in taking risks in new ways. Kung sees this as a central systemic issue for publishers: 'it is seductively inexpensive to produce a book' (2008:33) given oversupply of content and cheap production costs. This systemic attitude to risk is represented within the publishing workflow, which is designed to overproduce cheaply and efficiently.

Digital development also recognises that products may fail, but the approach to development is more iterative; the cost basis of experimenting with new digital products is different, and so the approach to risk needs to be different. One of the questions of the research is how far the current approach to new product development, even though it has a specific approach to risk and failure, is sustainable when considering digital innovation. New systems by which to experiment and measure failure may be required, as the current structure does not easily accommodate new ways of working.

Yet it is also significant that the print business in certain sectors remains large and key to a publishing business's operation. So while business structure can be seen as a legacy structure, it is still very successful for print output – new product development methods therefore are not required across the board, and any new approaches set up to experiment with digital products need to be integrated into a business without distorting the current processes that work effectively. Larger traditional publishers in particular have to deal with legacy cost structures in a way that does not disturb their large, existing marketplaces too much during transition.

Impact of digital transformation on publishing

As already noted, digital transformation impacts different functions within publishing. Digital publishing means many things, from content management systems and production processes to ebook formats and social media marketing; Maxwell says: 'technology is often assessed in terms of outputs but it is also important to attend to the transformations it brings about' (2019:328).

Technology allows for easy and quick dissemination across the internet so that distribution structures change; it allows content to be manipulated in different ways that can change the way it is consumed, and it leads to new methods of workflow that bring speed and flexibility to production (Bhaskar, 2013; Kasdorf, 2003; Maxwell, 2019; Phillips, 2014; Thompson, 2005). In addition, new methods of digital marketing can be used to promote new-style digital products, as well as print products, while digital analytics can inform marketing practice (Baverstock et al., 2015). New business models can be introduced, as pricing mechanisms can be adapted easily for markets with different purchasing patterns, and indeed this can help develop new markets (Dosdoce.com, 2015; Simon and de Prato, 2012; Steiner, 2018; Tian and Martin, 2011).

Change in publishing has tracked the wider media sector. Much has been written about the impacts of digital transformation on the content industries – for instance, around content abundance, convergence and blurred roles, downstream intermediaries, new concepts around reading as well as with converged media (Healy, 2011; Jenkins, 2006; Kung, 2016; Naughton, 2012; Scolari, 2009; Simon and Bogdanowicz, 2012; Weedon et al., 2014; Westin, 2013). Issues around copyright and intellectual property also arise, given the ease with which digital products can be disseminated, shared, reused and adapted (Healy, 2011; Hetherington, 2014; Jefferies and Kember, 2019; Jones and Benson, 2016; Nash, 2010; Naughton, 2012; Phillips, 2009).

While the industry has been adapting to the digital environment in terms of the sorts of products it makes, there has also been a significant change in the competitive environment in which it operates. New players from beyond the traditional publishing boundaries are starting to occupy publishing spaces. These players range from global technology corporations to small start-ups; the large companies like Apple, Google and Amazon come with financial and technological resources beyond the capacity of even large publishing companies (Steiner, 2018). The large technology companies control access to digital marketplaces through their devices and software, and, as new intermediaries, they can put pressure on publishers who want to reach their own consumer base. At the other end of the scale, small producers with lean and agile approaches are also having an effect: barriers to entering the market are reduced, and the cheapness of digital production and ease of using social media for marketing mean self-publishers can launch books and develop direct relationships with readers without the need for professional publishers (Baverstock et al., 2015). Fan fiction and other authoring sites can create alternative spaces for writers and readers to congregate (Davies, 2017; Hall, 2022; Jenkins, 2008). Publishers continue to develop their print businesses, bringing high-quality content to markets, but they may also need ways to develop new sorts of products that keep them relevant to new styles of consumers, whose patterns of consumption are being determined by the newer players.

Stages of digital development

While many commentators have explored the issues around the production of digital products (Healy, 2011; Michaels, 2015; Nash, 2010; Phillips, 2009, 2014; Scolari, 2019; Tian and Martin, 2011), the earlier stages in the development of digital technologies are not always considered. In the literature there is often an emphasis on the development of digital consumer titles, which was dependent on the development of effective e-readers, e-reading software, tablets and apps; but this can distract from the fact that, in specialist areas of publishing, the technology to produce digital products has been used for far longer.

Thompson proposes a four-stage model. The first stage was introduction of back-office systems that enable, for instance, bibliographic data to be produced, stored and transferred; these systems, in themselves, had an important impact within the related distribution and retail industries, first in physical and then in online form. The development of desktop publishing, content management systems and XML workflows followed; these have been important in managing, storing and producing content, allowing publishers to produce many sorts of products from one data set (Rech, 2012; Tian and Martin, 2011, 2013). The third stage is centred on marketing and services, with new sales intermediaries, social web and data analytics emerging. This leads to an unprecedented connectivity for publishers with their market, potentially turning them into 'service organisations, embedded in networks of communication' (Thompson, 2005:315). The fourth stage tackles the development of digital products in terms of content delivery (2005) with the emergence of new formats and platforms for readers; while the digital product is evolving in these four stages, reflecting a transformation whereby every aspect of the publishing process has been impacted from input of manuscript to output of product.

There are two significant things to note here. The first is that this is not a linear system of digital evolution. The digital book is not the end point of this process, and each of these four areas is continuously developing and can impact print as much as digital products; changes in all these areas can impact the way new products evolve. The second is that digital allows for more market-led publishing – the agility of process and flexibility in outputs means that products can be created and suited more directly to what the market needs at any one time, in any particular context.

In essence the function-oriented workflow is a product-led system (of course, still based on market research), but digital technologies allow products to be customised to the market, and it is the market that needs to shape them in the first place. With technology a wider variety of product design, for lower quantity and cost, becomes manageable, so it is much more possible that it used to be to start with understanding market demand before any product concepts are developed. Richard Nash summarises this at a macro level when he cites Potter and Ellenberg in a *Wired* article: 'The 20th Century was about sorting out supply . . . the 21st is going to be about sorting out demand' (Nash, 2010:116).

Contexts, containers and ecosystems

Similar to this is the concept of the context-first approaches rather than containers (O'Leary, 2011). The container – such as the print book – has long been the defining feature of published content (indeed, consumers felt that ebooks should be cheaper on the basis that the physical print cost something), but O'Leary argues that content should be defined not by the containers that it is possible to make, but rather by an understanding of the context and how the content will be used. Bhaskar's view that one of the roles of publishers is to frame and amplify content (2013, 2019) also develops the notion that publishing is not about the pre-determined output: this definition can encompass digital publishing as much as print publishing – reaching a neutral definition of what published content is. Both O'Leary and Bhaskar point to a vulnerability in publishing that looks towards the end point of a process, rather than through market-led publishing. In this sense the business model holds legacy elements which can hinder experimentation.

Ray Murray and Squires (2013), as they review the communications circuit in light of digital impacts, recognise that the challenge for newer digital business models is how to make them sustainable. How can concepts for crowdfunding, for instance, be developed to produce long-term publishing models rather than transitory experiments? The publisher Unbound is perhaps an example of how this can be achieved, through continuing to innovate around the business model. In this sense the answer lies in undertaking greater innovation and remaining agile in order to do so. Building on this is the notion of ecosystems in publishing (Simon and De Prato, 2012). The concept of an ecosystem for content industries is summarised by Naughton (2012), who, drawing on Marshall McLuhan, states: 'a community of organisations, publishers, authors, end users and audiences along with their environment that function together as a unit' (2012:114). This has some relationship with the digital communications circuit, and implicit in Naughton's summary is the expectation that things will evolve and develop organically. The development of digital products, even though it is still a smaller market than for print, is disruptive; as Simon and de Prato suggest, 'as [digital] is at the core of concerns of all actors in the book world, it disrupts the whole book ecosystem' (2012:71). Publishers recognise a changing relationship between different parts of the value chain: they observe that there is 'loss, creation and transfer of value [along the chain] and industry restructuring' (2012:72). This highlights the interconnectedness of aspects of the industry along a traditional value chain, and the way these relationships are having to readjust around digital transformation. The old ecosystem, then, is declining; but as Ray Murray and Squires show, new ones are emerging (2013). The wider ecosystem is perhaps gaining greater relevance as publishers' strategies diverge and they look for new partners and relationships.

Digital innovation – on the ground

The amount of experimentation that went on earlier in the cycle of digital transformation has to some extent been reduced. The industry has responded to market change and tried out new products which, in some cases, have been ahead of the market, with new format ideas coming too early for a consumer that is only beginning to change. For example, John Makinson in 2011 reported on the effects of the Stephen Fry releases in various digital forms, reflecting that the market was not in actuality ready for all these products (the print version still outstripping the other digital versions) but stating that at Penguin, the 'appetite for experimentation was undiminished' (Reuters, 2011). Publishers have been quick to explore new business models, such as the creative commons approach taken by Bloomsbury Academic, or digital-only imprints for genre-based areas such as romance, which have now been running for some years. Joint ventures such as the e-retail book club site Anobii were ultimately sold off to mainstream web retailers, while other new ideas like Authonomy, a HarperCollins reader-writer community site, that offered an innovative approach to content acquisition dwindled. Projects like Black Crown at Random House had good reviews and creative success, but were challenging to support and financially unprofitable so ultimately had to close (Shaffi, 2014). These experiments reflect on an industry understanding the need to move and try things out.

Some digital experiments work: ebooks, as a replica of a book, obviously do well; digital-only imprints are prevalent, and genre-based publishing is in particular experimenting effectively here; hybrid publishing is also growing on the back of self-publishing trends (Hall, 2022). However, creativity in new product formats has idled. A failed experiment does not necessarily lead to the next one, which is a challenge. There have been, within industry events, regular calls for the industry to learn how to experiment effectively; for instance, Nash said: 'Fail fast and fail cheap', while author Neil Gaiman stated at the same event: 'The model for tomorrow is try everything, make mistakes, fail, fail better' (Jones, 2013).

This approach would be more recognisable within technology development: publishing is limited in that there is often less finance available for experiments compared to technology companies. However, it is also both a reason for more collaborations, to help manage the risk effectively, as well as new ways of developing products that are tested in iterative ways and are not regarded as 'complete' as a finite print book (or its ebook equivalent). Accommodating this ongoing approach to production processes requires another sort of change in the workflow, while understanding new product development approaches requires organisational change.

Mini-case study survey – on impacts of digital change

As outlined in the Introduction, an initial survey helped to establish which aspects of digital transformation are particularly concerning the industry. This asked industry leaders about the ways in which they felt digital was impacting their businesses and the organisational responses that they might need to develop. In terms of functions, it was clear most aspects of publishing were impacted in some way by digital change. The issues though that were most significant centred on legacy (of processes, structures and models) and the challenges posed by big tech; other issues emerged such as copyright or skills gaps, but of primary concern were those that reflected more structural challenges. Specific things like OA continue to evolve, but the industry has well-established processes of ongoing development around OA, while other issues such as early DRM have receded (Hall, 2022).

However, what was significant was that most of the participants felt that structural change was necessary and that there needed to be flexible approaches that moved away from what one participant described as 'institutional conservatism'. This reflected a broad recognition that change was now continual, not just cyclical, and that the industry needed to develop a responsive and agile approach. They appeared to share a vision for publishing in a digital age and recognised the requirements to shape a business effectively for this. Their vision centres on working with others to collaborate on new projects, learn new skills and take up opportunities to restructure in order to respond to digital developments in the future; and they see that they must continue to focus on the core strength of creating and managing content. This suggests a dynamism across the industry to take action in light of change, and to keep innovating in different ways (Hall, 2016).

In terms of ways to achieve this, the survey showed that most companies were doing the following: reviewing company structure, looking at skill sets, carrying out more collaborations and partnerships, developing new strategies for content development and reviewing business models. Collaboration emerged as one of the key responses of the industry to the digital environment. The survey started to delve into this further, beginning to categorise a new type of collaboration which could lead to new content approaches and which is distinct from older-style transactional collaborations. This part of the research surprisingly concluded that collaboration sat at the heart of responses to digital change; it was regarded as critical to collaborate more with a wider range of partners. This pointed to aspects of diversity as well as tapping into a wider range of expertise and creative skills.

Interesting points emerged from the survey about the way the creativity is shared between collaborators. The drive for creativity in innovation leads to the requirement to work with partners in particular ways, sharing work practices, trusting each other and developing new ideas together. Comments related to the way companies select and work with partners: one participant noted, 'Partners [are] chosen significantly because of cultural fit and alignment – i.e. do we work quickly and effectively together, so we trust each other?' Another comment reflected that collaboration leads to different sorts of results – 'we are getting much more input on the end product' – while one participant pointed to the fact that one might be connecting with competitors in order to explore new ideas: 'what is interesting to me is different types of collaboration e.g. between formerly competing . . . suppliers to create global networks'.

These requirements can determine the choice of partners as publishers look for people they can work with effectively. The survey suggested too that, once collaborative partners are connected, the behaviour of the partnership is also important, as it impacts speed of operation and levels of risk taking for innovation. The collaborative work the participants pointed to were more open, experimental projects, with less defined outcomes, reflecting more of a process for innovation.

Conclusion

The structures of publishing developed and honed over many decades have led to organisations that are perhaps not as flexible and opportunistic as it might need to be to tackle the challenges posed by rapid digital change. Legacy structures have limitations that are increasingly apparent even while publishing seeks to be innovative; this is observable not just in traditional workflows, but in business models and attitudes to risk. The industry, however, does not work in isolation but forms part of a set of creative industries that operate in similar ways. The survey showed that publishers are looking to make connections with a wider range of partners, including other parts of the creative sector. Some of the characteristics of these industries reflect a particular way of working that, in effect, facilitates connectivity, creativity and collaboration. Publishers have partnered with different parts of these industries before, on a more transactional basis where, for instance, they buy in content or brand projects. But it appears these industries could provide opportunities to do more. It is this link to the wider creative industries and the way they collaborate that is explored next.

References

Baverstock, A., Blackburn, R., Iskandarova, M., (2015) How the role of the independent editor is changing in relation to traditional and self-publishing. *Learned Publishing* 28, 123–131. https://doi.org/10.1087/20150206

Bhaskar, M., (2013) *The content machine: Towards a theory of publishing from the printing press to the digital network.* London: Anthem Press.

Bhaskar, M., (2019) Are publishers worth it? Filtering, amplification and the value of publishing, in: *Whose book is it anyway?* London: Open Book Publishers, pp. 91–104.

Coser, L.A., (1975) Publishers as gatekeepers of ideas. *The Annals of the American Academy of Political and Social Science* 421, 14–22.

Darnton, R., (2002) What is the history of books? in: Finklestein, D., (Ed.), *The book history reader.* Abingdon: Routledge.

Darnton, R., (2010) *The case for books: Past, present, and future.* New York: Public Affairs.

Davies, R., (2017) Collaborative production and the transformation of publishing, in: Graham J., Gandini A. (Eds.) *Collaborative Production in the*

Creative Industries. London: Westminster University Press, pp. 51–67. https://doi.org/10.16997/book4.d

Dosdoce.com, (2015) *New business models in the digital age*. http://book machine.org/product/new-business-models-in-the-digital-age/

Hall, F., (2016) Digital change and industry responses: Exploring organisational and strategic issues in the book-publishing industry. *Logos* 27, 19–31. https://doi.org/10.1163/1878-4712-11112102

Hall, F., (2019) Organizational Structures in Publishing, in Bhaskar. M.,Phillips, A, (eds.) *The Oxford Handbook of Publishing*. Oxford: OUP.

Hall, F., (2022) *The business of digital publishing: An introduction to the digital book and journal industries*. Abingdon: Routledge.

Healy, M., (2011) Seeking permanence in a time of turbulence. *Logos* 22, 7–15. https://doi.org/10.1163/095796511x580275

Hetherington, D., (2014) Book publishing: New environments call for new operating models. *Publishing Research Quarterly* 30, 382–387. https://doi.org/10.1007/s12109-014-9379-y

Hirsch, P.M., (1972) Processing fads and fashions: An organization-set analysis of cultural industry systems. *American Journal of Sociology* 77, 639–659.

Jefferies, J., Kember, S., (2019) *Whose book is it anyway? View from elsewhere on publishing, copyright and creativity*. London: Open Book Publishers.

Jenkins, H., (2006) *Convergence culture: Where old and new media collide*. New York: NYU Press.

Jones, H., Benson, C., (2016) *Publishing law*. Abingdon: Routledge.

Jones, P., (2013) *Digital minds: Industry must try more, fail better*. www.thebookseller.com/news/digital-minds-industry-must-try-more-fail-better

Kasdorf, W.E., (2003) *The Columbia guide to digital publishing*. New York: Columbia University Press.

Kung, L., (2008) *Strategic management in the media*, 2nd Edn. London: Sage.

Kung, L., (2016) *Strategic management in the media: Theory to practice*, 2nd Edn. London: Sage.

Maxwell, J., (2019) Publishing and technology, in: *The Oxford handbook of publishing*. Oxford: Oxford University Press.

Michaels, K., (2015) The evolving challenges and opportunities in global publishing. *Publishing Research Quarterly* 31, 1–8. https://doi.org/10.1007/s12109-014-9392-1

Murray, P.R., Squires, C., (2013) The digital publishing communications circuit. *Book 2.0* 3, 3–23. https://doi.org/10.1386/btwo.3.1.3_1

Nash, R., (2010) Publishing 2020. *Publishing Research Quarterly* 26, 114–118. https://doi.org/10.1007/s12109-010-9155-6

Naughton, J., (2012) *From Gutenberg to Zuckerberg: What you really need to know about the internet*. London: Quercus.

Negus, K.R., (2002) The work of cultural intermediaries and the enduring distance between production and consumption. *Cultural Studies* 16, 501–515. https://doi.org/10.1080/09502380210139089

O'Leary, B.F., (2011) Context first: A unified field theory of publishing. *Publishing Research Quarterly* 27, 211–219. https://doi.org/10.1007/s12109-011-9221-8

Phillips, A., (2009) Does the book have a future? in: *A companion to the history of the book*. Chichester: Wiley-Blackwell, pp. 547–559.

Phillips, A., (2014) *Turning the page: The evolution of the book*. Abingdon: Routledge.

Porter, M.E., (1985) *Competitive advantage: Creating and sustaining superior performance*. New York: Free Press

Rech, D.A., (2012) Instituting an xml-first workflow. *Publishing Research Quarterly* 28, 192–196. https://doi.org/10.1007/s12109-012-9278-z

Reuters, (2011) Penguin Learns Digital Lessons available at: http://uk.reuters.com/video/2013/09/24/penguin-learns-digital-lessons?videoId=225927220 (accessed 18/08/2015).

Scolari, C., (2009) Transmedia storytelling: Implicit consumers, narrative worlds, and branding in contemporary media production. *International Journal of Communication* 3, 586–606.

Scolari, C., (2019) Networks, in: *The Oxford handbook of publishing*. Oxford: Oxford University Press, pp. 127–146.

Shaffi, S., (2014) *PRH's Black Crown project to go offline*. www.thebookseller.com/news/prhs-black-crown-project-go-offline

Simon, J.P., Bogdanowicz, M., (2012) *The digital shift in the media and content industries: Policy brief (policy document no. 1/2013), EUR scientific and research series*. Luxembourg: European Commission.

Simon, J.P., De Prato, G., (2012) *Statistical, ecosystems and competitiveness analysis of the media and content industries: The book publishing industry*. Luxembourg: European Union.

Steiner, A., (2018) The Global book: Micropublishing, conglomerate production, and digital market structures. *Publishing Research Quarterly* 34, 118–132. https://doi.org/10.1007/s12109-017-9558-8

Thompson, J.B., (2005) *Books in the digital age: The transformation of academic higher education publishing in Britain and the United States*. Cambridge: Polity

Thompson, J.B., (2012) *Merchants of culture: The publishing business in the twenty-first century*. Cambridge: Polity

Tian, X., Martin, B., (2011) Impacting forces on ebook business models development. *Publishing Research Quarterly* 27, 230–246. https://doi.org/10.1007/s12109-011-9229-0

Tian, X., Martin, B., (2013) Value chain adjustments in educational publishing. *Publishing Research Quarterly* 29, 12–25. https://doi.org/10.1007/s12109-012-9303-2

Weedon, A., Miller, D., Franco, C.P., Moorhead, D., Pearce, S., (2014) Crossing media boundaries: Adaptations and new media forms of the book. *Convergence* 20, 108–124. https://doi.org/10.1177/1354856513515968

Westin, J., (2013) Loss of culture: New media forms and the translation from analogue to digital books. *Convergence* 19, 129–140. https://doi.org/10.1177/1354856512452398

3 Managing publishing as a creative business

Introduction

The aim of this chapter is to examine the position of publishing within the wider arena of the creative industries. Publishers recognise that they need to be collaborating with a broader range of organisations. Publishing currently contributes to the wider creative industries in the form of content development that flows into other sectors, such as TV, film and theatre, through book adaptations and marketing (Frontier Economics, 2018); they do this in transactional ways such as selling rights to book content. While this will continue, publishers are also likely to be developing different sorts of relationships with these creative sectors, working in ways that are more embedded as joint ventures. As the partners of the future may come from establishing more connections with these industries, it is useful to understand how publishing fits within this context. New-style collaborations may lead to innovation and experimentation, and through recognising their shared characteristics and management styles, partners can develop effective ways to work together.

Defining the creative industries

The concept of the creative industries emerged from an economic policy in the UK in 1998 as a way to summarise a group of industries that were regarded as important drivers of growth for the country (DCMS, 1998). It built on the notion of cultural industries but was framed to focus on the economic potential of these industries: they represent creative and media sectors that can create, monetise and potentially export products and services, stimulating wealth through jobs and skills development. The definitions of the creative industries and the cultural industries vary, but the latter more usually centred on arenas of cultural production such as art and books, theatre and museums (Bilton, 2006; Hesmondhalgh, 2013). The creative industries, however, can include media and service businesses such as advertising, which tend not to be included in groupings of cultural industries. The concept of the creative economy developed by Howkins (2001) is related to this, as he centres on

DOI: 10.4324/9781003378211-3

the link between the economic potential of these industries and their creative output (Bilton, 2006; Howkins, 2001); while creative industries may deliver other kinds of value too (such as cultural wealth or social capital) it is the potential for these industries to help economic growth that was particularly important (Howkins, 2001).

These industries include a variety of sectors ranging from very individualistic production of art, in the form of fine art, to global service providers such as major advertising corporations; it can include industries ranging in diversity from world heritage sites and tourism to product design and fashion. Trying to find suitable, all-encompassing definitions, therefore, can prove challenging. There are different ways of categorising creative industries, but they are not always satisfactory in accommodating both the cultural and commercial imperatives (or paradoxes) that are at the root of many creative industries (Banks and O'Connor, 2009; DeFillippi et al., 2007; Flew, 2013; Hall, 2014; Hesmondhalgh, 2013). Some of these models are explicitly about economic policy (e.g. DCMS, 1998). Others that are more academic in origin attempt to align the nature of creative value and the cultural importance of these industries (Throsby, 2008; Hesmondhalgh, 2013). It is difficult to draw links between very different industries, as they encompass so many things from local crafts to global gaming conglomerates; but attempts to model the industries are focused on trying to show that connections should be made in order to ensure these industries can be supported as a group, and also that they should connect to and support each other (Banks and O'Connor, 2009; DeFillippi et al., 2007).

Publishing has a place in all these models, although with varying degrees of centrality. It is, at times, seen to be more on the periphery as a disseminating business (Throsby, 2008), while it is more central in WIPO models because of the importance of intellectual property to the industry (2015). It is unclear as to the extent to which publishing sees itself as closely aligned with other creative industries, and these models tend to oversimplify (Bilton, 2006). Nevertheless, publishing needs to consider its relationship to the wider cultural economy more explicitly (Marsden, 2017). Positioning publishing in this wider context may allow greater recognition of the opportunities for collaboration.

Characteristics of creative industries

One way to explore publishing's relationship with the wider creative sector is to look at the characteristics it shares with other parts of the sector. This may lead to a better understanding of the behaviour of these industries and the opportunities and challenges of collaboration between them. These shared characteristics can be summarised as follows:

•   Issues around value, cultural production and symbolic texts
•   Distinctive market behaviours

- Work/experience of labour/working conditions, including network behaviour
- Management and organisational practices

Value of cultural texts

The first characteristic that is reflected across many sectors of the creative industries is the way cultural products are valued. The concept of value is open for debate in itself; the value to society of the aesthetic sensitivity and the societal commentary vested in cultural texts is important to consider, as is the operation of value and its fluctuation within the unique structural behaviour of the field of cultural production (Bourdieu, 1993). When considering who has the ability to say something has artistic merit (artist, critic, audience, etc.), the 'gatekeeper' (Bourdieu, 1993; Hirsch, 1972) emerges as a key term, reflecting the need to select and curate the best of our cultural texts (Bhaskar, 2016; Hesmondhalgh, 2013); the 'gatekeeper', however, is a term that has become more problematic since the rise of the internet (Naughton, 2012), given its implication of restriction. The gatekeeper perhaps segues into Bhaskar's concept of curation which explores aspects of discovering quality amid abundance (2016), while Thompson's symbolic value (2012) recognises that cultural value and economic value may be different. Who decides on value remains, therefore, a consideration for any creative industry producing what might be regarded as a cultural text.

Building on this point, the sector as a whole is often typified by the central dilemma regarding the balance between cultural value and profit. The art and commerce debate (Ryan's 'art-commerce relation', 1992, cited in Banks and O'Connor, 2009) is in itself something that reflects a special characteristic of the creative industries and that particularly engages debate in publishing (Caves, 2003; Kung, 2016; Bérubé and Gauthier, 2023).

Most publishing has some sort of financial imperative in order to break even, whether aiming to produce cultural texts or not, and very little is entirely subsidised. Yet publishing, along with other creative industries, is also seen to be doing something important for society, either in the form of entertainment or for information and education; for this reason, it is an industry around which certain specific rules may apply (over sales tax, for instance). This illustrates a tension between its commercial necessities and its artistic relevance. This somewhat uncomfortable connection can be recognised across the creative industries and so reflect a connection between publishing and other sectors. This dichotomy may well be reflected in the collaborations: for instance, one of the case studies explores an arts organisation and a publisher who both share a similar need to make money while also educating and entertaining. It also impacts how these industries measure the success given these two imperatives.

Distinctive market behaviours

The next issue establishes that characteristic market and economic behaviours can be identified in the way the market works for creative sectors. Bourdieu (1993) unpicks the field of cultural production at one level in terms of assessing value, but there are specific ways in which each sector may operate – from the artist using exhibitions to showcase their work, to advertising agencies developing new business through beauty parades. Hirsch (1972) identifies systems around publishing activities that, for example, combine filtering with producing surplus, and that make use of intelligence agents at the input and output (from talent scouts to bookshop reps). Thompson (2012) also illustrates the structural nature of the industry as he observes various activities within the value chain that seem to be more characteristic of creative businesses compared to other industries. Balancing risk and supply in particular ways is critical to creative industries where it is difficult to predict success (Davies and Sigthorsson, 2013; Hirsch, 1972). Publishers are familiar with these market behaviours, as are other creative industries, and so reflect shared characteristics that can help when collaborating.

The nature of creative work and importance of networks

The nature of the work, as particularly studied by Hesmondhalgh and Baker (2011), focuses on the experience of the individual and the characteristics of their work. These characteristics include project-based work that is often dependent on people freelancing. There is a precariousness combined with glamour to the work, and those who participate in the industry are often accustomed to portfolio careers where they may enjoy the benefits of autonomy but also may have to accept low pay; they may even see themselves as making a sacrifice for the sense of doing 'good' work (Banks et al., 2009; Bilton, 2006; Graham and Gandini, 2017; Gandini et al., 2017; Hesmondhalgh and Baker, 2011; McRobbie, 2016).

These characteristics will be as familiar to those involved in publishing as other creative sectors, involving as it does many freelance activities ranging from copy editors to designers. There is within publishing an interplay between the overall publishing business and the various projects within it; creative labour is managed sometimes around the publishing business and sometimes around the project (Kung, 2008; Sigthorsson and Davies, 2013). Because work fluctuates for those involved between busy periods and periods with no projects, having strong networks in order to find the next project is important (Bilton, 2006; Blair, 2003; Hesmondhalgh and Baker, 2011; Starkey et al., 2000). Many in publishing, therefore, are familiar with the project-based behaviour of their activity and so are used to working in a collaborative way because it is fundamental to their practice. The sector also recognises the importance of networks for making the connections that lead to the next project or collaboration which will be explored in later chapters.

Management through projects

The previous point reflects the creative working for the individual. There is also a characteristic for these industries that centres on the wider context of work in exploring management styles and managing creative processes and creative people. This builds on an understanding of organisational behaviour, where organisational and company networks feature strongly in project formation and execution. Organisations need to work flexibly and engender an entrepreneurialism in order to develop new creative projects (Bilton, 2006; Flew, 2013; Gandini et al., 2017). Yet specific projects do need results: Bérubé and Gauthier (2023) note that creative projects require compromises between traditional management techniques and artistic values, mediated by a project manager; there is tension between styles of management, whereby projects need to be clearly defined around timelines and outcomes but are flexible enough to allow for creative inspiration.

Here publishing can clearly be seen as sharing the characteristics of other parts of the sector; whether a project is drawn together from within a company or makes greater use of freelancers, whether it is an author and illustrator with a small publishing team or a very specific project team gathered to start up a large new online reference project, the publishing industry is used to working in a project-based way. This trend appears to be growing further in strength within publishing, and it is having a more fundamental impact on publishing structures, as some publishers are reconfiguring to allow for further management of project-based product innovation. For instance, several publishers in recent years have focused on developing outsourced, contract-based teams that can expand and contract around projects. Industries share creative project management practices because of their project-based activity.

Other characteristics

Other characteristics are recognisable across the industries. In various places across the sector, cultural production is diverging between conglomerates (such as global media companies) and grassroots producers who are combining entrepreneurial and craft approaches to creation (Davies and Sigthorsson, 2013; Graham and Gandini, 2017; Jenkins, 2006). Evidence of that can be seen in publishing, where large companies believe in the importance of merging in order to retain some power in the marketplace (e.g. Penguin and Random House), while others focus on the niche (e.g. ebook-only publishers of genre fiction) and the crafted product (with specialists like Visual Editions or Persephone books). There are other shared characteristics such as cultures of making, connecting and sharing cultures (Gauntlett, 2011) and gift economies (Davies and Sigthorsson, 2013). Issues around government cultural policy and urban planning through creative clusters also link these industries.

Creative industries and shared challenges

Having mapped recognised characteristics of creative industries onto the publishing industry, it can also be useful to map challenges publishing faces back to the wider creative industries; The same problems are testing many parts of the industry in similar ways. It may be that these shared challenges are, in part, a driver for these industries to collaborate more frequently as they attempt to find effective and cost-efficient ways to develop innovative products and to be entrepreneurial. Many areas of concern that publishers now face can very easily be recognised in other creative industries.

Copyright

Discussions around copyright, particularly its ability to function in a digital environment, resonate in a number of areas for the publishing industry, whether open access or the Google settlement (Darnton, 2010; Hall, 2022). Similar discussions exist around copyright in other industries specifically (e.g. music, or reuse of people's artworks). There are most abstract debates about the nature of intellectual property giving rise to issues including freedom for creators to share easily (Lessig, 2004), freedom for fans to enjoy their favourite characters (Jenkins, 2006) and democratic issues around ownership on the internet and gatekeepers (Lanier, 2011; Leadbeater, 2009; Naughton, 2012). In this way copyright control can be linked to the restrictive impact of gatekeepers. There is the possibility that while the internet should be a collaborative space, the creative industry professional may in fact be regarded as a controlling, destructive, economically motivated force that prevents creation and sharing by aggressively protecting copyright (Jenkins, 2006; Shirky, 2008). Yet copyright remains central to many creative industries as an embodiment of their creativity and their commitment to developing and adding value for the creator; they face a challenge to ensure this is understood properly and can lead to positive creative production.

New consumer behaviours

Changes in consumer behaviour are faced by many creative sectors; product ownership is replaced by licensing, micro payments around usage substitute one-off transactions and service and subscription models become more commonplace (Tzuo and Weisert, 2018). In these cases, the value of content changes in relation to the value of access. The actual content is potentially commoditised (as illustrated by the Google book scanning project; Darnton, 2010). This issue is recognisable across many industries including publishing, film and music (Bilton, 2006; Healy, 2011; Jenkins, 2006; Kung, 2008). This sort of change can be a driver to collaboration, as creative sectors need to find new ways to produce content that are directed to a new generation of consumers (McKinsey, 2019; OC&C, 2019). Here collaboration may allow these industries to share resources and information to develop new formats that cater to new consumers, recognising that these challenges may be more effectively faced together.

Discoverability

With access potentially unlimited and the opportunity for DIY creative production, making products findable is a challenge across many creative industries. Creative products can find opportunities related to the long tail but also face challenges in making their niche findable (Anderson, 2008). 'Publish then filter' (Shirky, 2008) also reflects a changing consumer who expects to have access to everything and then decide upon and filter what they need for themselves. Similarly, the demise of the expert reviewer (or reinvention among the crowd) adds to problems of discoverability (Jenkins, 2006). This is an additional challenge for publishers looking to develop digital formats, as they may have to make their products findable in new arenas such as app stores. Collaboration can help things become more discoverable, whether sharing expertise amongst partners about promoting content, spreading content into different publishing channels, aggregating content with competitors to gain critical mass or crossing media boundaries to ensure greater accessibility from all angles.

Prosumer

The prosumer (Toffler, 1970) who produces and consumes without the need for specialist creative intermediaries has been touched on already (Deuze, 2007; Leadbeater, 2009). For some prosumer activity, the only intermediaries required are the global technology companies who produce the creation and distribution tools (such as Adobe) and control platforms for distribution (such as Kindle) (Gauntlett, 2011; Rushkoff, 2011; Shirky, 2008). From self-publishing to viewers of YouTube, producers and consumers easily merge and bypass creative distributors, which is a challenge many of the creative sectors face; this reflects the requirement of the sector to continue to innovate as well as embrace the new style of consumer.

The new competitor landscape

As a result of disintermediation, new competitors from outside the creative industries have started to enter the arena. The new entrants, such as Amazon, Apple and Google, have different visions and valuation of content (Hall, 2022; Steiner, 2018). Content for them is a subset to their work rather than their main activity, yet they can command immense resources and can afford to undertake activity within creative sectors without the same commercial imperatives faced by creative companies. Creative industries may need to collaborate in order to compete with these much larger companies that are operating in very different ways from the creative industries. Competitors are an important driver for strategic partnerships and collaborations.

The changing business landscape, accelerated by digital transformation, is having an impact on all the creative industries. Challenges around copyright, discoverability, new style consumers and new competitors are all issues emerging as a result of the changing digital environment and the opportunities and threats it brings. To face these challenges, collaboration will be central.

Strategy and management for creative industries

Being creative and effectively managing creativity processes sit at the heart of all these industries. The final part of this chapter focuses on the ways they can do this though their management and organisational structures; this is of relevance when considering the way collaborations can be facilitated, which in turn can stimulate innovative practices.

Flexible organisational structures

One of the central features of the creative sector is the way it manages creativity to ensure it is continuously innovative. Creativity, according to Bilton, is the sector's central ingredient: 'the way in which creative processes, talents and products are managed and developed in the creative industries are distinctive and these are working methods and models that are worth studying' (2006:20). While his study is from the mid-2000s, predating more recent digital change, Bilton's analysis of the organisational behaviour of the creative industries brings to the fore some of the fundamental aspects of management theory when mapped to creativity, such as flexibility and autonomy; these are still relevant today because of the increased need to focus on continuous innovation in a constantly changing environment. Hierarchical, rigid organisations do not always suit knowledge creation, which requires interaction and knowledge exchange; whereas flexible structures make more sense for the fast-moving development of innovative products, where highly skilled, talent-oriented workforces can be easily redeployed and mobilised quickly to respond to market changes.

However, the value chain approach to business organisations, whereby value is added at each stage of a standardised production process, is a potential limiting factor. Value chains simplify creativity, as can be seen in publishing: creativity exists in the initial input into the value chain (different authors, for example) but then follows a finely tuned and highly effective, but predictable production process, repeated again and again for each new title. Yet creativity is 'unpredictable and discontinuous' (Bilton, 2006:xvii) and is required to respond quickly to face challenges in new ways. There remains a question, therefore, as to whether the structures in some areas of the publishing sector are flexible enough in a period of fast digital change: here legacy systems can limit innovation, in particular innovation in digital formats which require different development and production processes.

Ecosystems and the process of creativity

If creativity can be embedded further into the behaviour of an organisation, through its structure and management, then that may improve the sector's responses to the challenges it faces (Bilton, 2006; Kung, 2016). Organisational creativity is concerned with making connections between individuals and organisations within a creative network or 'system' (Bilton, 2006:49). Publishing has its own ecosystem, but the wider creative industries can also be seen as ecosystems, not just because each sector has its own patterns and protocols around the way it behaves, nor because networks that give rise to creativity are 'delicate ecosystems' in themselves, but because creativity as a whole can be seen as a process or system.

This counters the 'genius' approach to creativity, where creativity stems from one talented individual or is in other ways inspirational, unpredictable and so unmanageable. Rather, creativity is a process that can be managed (Bilton, 2006; Kung, 2008, 2016; Sawyer, 2017); 'creativity is dependent upon the relationships between individuals and organisations, not the competencies within individuals and organisations' (Bilton, 2006:53). This has important implications for the network and collaborative activity, as it suggests that creativity itself is embedded in the connections and relationships of the organisations; the industry therefore can instil practices that encourage creativity, not just rely on creative individuals. Publishing may regard the author as their key source of new ideas, but the research into creativity management shows that the ecosystems inside the publishing house and its network of connections with other creative sectors can also be a source of creativity.

Innovation itself can be viewed as a business process whereby creativity is situated in the organisation in formal ways (Amabile, 1988; Kung, 2008). As such, everyday management practices can be put in place to foster creativity: these include developing work environments that encourage autonomy, committing resources to experimentation, setting up challenges and assessing effective team composition (Kung, 2016). The process of creativity therefore can be built into collaborative and creative projects themselves and into the wider organisational structure.

Managing creative teams

Managing creative teams effectively is one of the central ways the industry manages creativity. Recognising the importance of team make-up for incubating creativity is important; as Bilton says, creativity depends on

> assembling different components – different styles of thinking, different processes and ideas different contexts – in unexpected combinations. It is

the combination of innovation and value that in the end is both surprising and satisfying, achieved through a combination of spontaneous inventiveness and laborious preparation.

(2006:5).

Team diversity is therefore important for creativity, and this will continue to emerge later in the exploration of nature of collaboration. The compromises between artistic values and project techniques also need to be continuously negotiated (Bérubé and Gauthier, 2023), reflecting the way diverse teams need to be flexible in practice.

These teams need some level of autonomy to allow them to be truly creative (Bilton, 2006; Kung, 2016; Sawyer, 2017). This is important for being able to do things differently, to adopt new strategies and redirect resources. The size of the team can be significant too: it can be easier for larger organisations to give smaller teams the freedom they need to be experimental, what Kung calls 'small-scale autonomy' (2008:221).

Even where autonomy can be managed within a collaboration, there needs to be a link to the parent organisations, where the resources to develop the idea into a sustainable proposition lie. Effectively managing change becomes key to the business's ability to adapt and evolve in order to absorb the new developments; Kung too points to the need to recognise the balance between the autonomy to be creative and the management processes required to bring a project to fruition (2008). This leads to the expectation that each collaboration will have its own ecosystem in order to navigate this: it will need systems in place to be able to be creative effectively, to harness diversity and ensure connectivity while also being flexible and autonomous so as to be open to new ideas and able to act on them. The case studies will examine how the collaborations manage to achieve this balance.

Managing change in the creative sector

These sorts of processes for stimulating innovation are central to the creative value of an organisation, particularly in times of change; change in this case is reflected in the rapid digital transformation of the industries. The need for creativity and innovation is 'enlarged when environments become unstable' (Kung, 2008:63). If creative industries are facing challenges, such as the emergence of new competitors or prosumers, developing further methods for more creative and innovative activity will be important; this becomes a way to navigate change.

Effective change management is important, as the creative industries need to respond quickly to environmental changes. Embedding structural and systematic approaches to change are important; furthermore, creating an environment capable of dealing effectively with change on an ongoing basis is key, rather than moving awkwardly between change cycles (Kung, 2016). Change needs to be managed in a gradual and experimental way rather than as a reaction to a crisis; continuous, adaptive strategies are key, as is being proactive and incremental (Bilton, 2006).

Collaboration in this context could be one of several adaptive strategies that help an organisation face change as a way of embedding an innovation system. Collaborations require freedom and autonomy to be creative as well as formal management practices to be sustainable.

Conclusion

This chapter presented ways of thinking about publishing in relation to the wider creative industries. By recognising shared characteristics and shared challenges, these industries may be able to come together to develop collaborative approaches to competition and innovation. Creativity can be managed; this happens through flexible organisation, creative ecosystems, autonomous teams and divergent thinking. These features are becoming more central to a creative organisation's response during a period of increasingly rapid change, allowing the organisation to harness creativity for new product development. By working with the wider creative industries, publishers can find allies from whom they can learn; bringing together diverse people from across the sector also offers new ways of collaborating. Current publishing structures can limit the sort of flexible approaches to innovation required. Kung states, 'creating an organisation that combines the free space for small groups to be creative, unencumbered by bureaucracy, with the resources and infrastructure needed to finance and support successful products represents a tremendous challenge' (2008:216). The case studies will be tested to see how successfully they manage this balance between the small agile group and the wider creative organisation.

References

Amabile, T.M., (1988) A model of creativity and innovation in organisations. *Research in Organisational Behaviour* 10, 123–67.

Anderson, C., (2008) *The long tail: Why the future of business is selling less of more*. New York: Hyperion

Banks, M., O'Connor, J., (2009) After the creative industries. *International Journal of Cultural Policy* 15, 365–373. https://doi.org/10.1080/10286630902989027

Bérubé, J., Gauthier, J.-B., (2023) Managing projects in creative industries: A compromise between artistic and project management values. *Creative Industries Journal* 16, 76–95. https://doi.org/10.1080/17510694.2021.1979278

Bhaskar, M., (2016) *Curation: The power of selection in a world of excess*. London: Hachette.

Bilton, C., (2006) *Management and creativity: From creative industries to creative management*. Chichester: John Wiley & Sons.

Blair, H., (2003) Winning and losing in flexible labour markets: The formation and operation of networks of interdependence in the UK film industry. *Sociology* 37, 677–694. https://doi.org/10.1177/00380385030374003

Bourdieu, P., (1993) *The field of cultural production: Essays on art and literature*. New York: Columbia University Press

Caves, R.E., (2003) Contracts between art and commerce. *Journal of Economic Perspectives* 17, 73–83. https://doi.org/10.1257/089533003765888430

Darnton, R., (2010) *The case for books: Past, present, and future*. New York: PublicAffairs.

Davies, R., Sigthorsson, G., (2013) *Introducing the creative industries: From theory to practice*. London: Sage.

DCMS, (1998) *Creative industries mapping documents 1998*. www.gov.uk/government/publications/creative-industries-mapping-documents-1998

DeFillippi, R., Grabher, G., Jones, C., (2007) Paradoxes of creativity: Managerial and organizational challenges in the cultural economy. *Journal of Organizational Behavior* 28, 511–521.

Deuze, M., (2007) Convergence culture in the creative industries. *International Journal of Cultural Studies* 10, 243–263. https://doi.org/10.1177/1367877907076793

Flew, T., (2013) *Global creative industries, global media and communication*. Cambridge: Polity.

Frontier Economics, (2018) *Publishing's contribution to the wider creative industries: A report prepared for the Publishers Association*. London: The Publishers Association.

Gandini, A., Bandinelli, C., Cossu, A., (2017) Collaborating, competing, co-working, coalescing: Artists, freelancers and social entrepreneurs as the 'new subjects' of the creative economy, in: Gandini, A., Graham, J., (Eds.). *Collaborative Production in the Creative Industries*, London: University of Westminster Press, pp. 15–32. https://doi.org/10.16997/book4.b

Gauntlett, D., (2011) *Making is connecting: The social meaning of creativity, from DIY and Knitting to YouTube and Web 2.0*. Cambridge: Polity.

Graham, J., Gandini, A., (2017) Introduction: Collaborative production in the creative industries, in: Gandini, A., Graham, J., (Eds.). *Collaborative Production in the Creative Industries*, London: University of Westminster Press, pp. 1–14. https://doi.org/10.16997/book4.a

Hall, F., (2014) Digital convergence and collaborative cultures. *Logos* 25, 20–31. https://doi.org/10.1163/1878-4712-11112055

Hall, F., (2022) *The business of digital publishing: An introduction to the digital book and journal industries*. Abingdon: Routledge.

Healy, M., (2011) Seeking permanence in a time of turbulence. *Logos* 22, 7–15. https://doi.org/10.1163/095796511x580275

Hesmondhalgh, D., (2013) *The cultural industries*, 3rd Edn. London: Sage.

Hesmondhalgh, D., Baker, S., (2011) *Creative labour: Media work in three cultural industries*. London: Routledge.

Hirsch, P.M., (1972) Processing fads and fashions: An organization-set analysis of cultural industry systems. *American Journal of Sociology* 77, 639–659.

Howkins, J., (2001) *The creative economy: How people make money from ideas*. London: Allen Lane.

Jenkins, H., (2006) *Convergence culture: Where old and new media collide*. New York: NYU Press.

Kung, L., (2008) *Strategic management in the media*. London: Sage.

Kung, L., (2016) *Strategic management in the media: Theory to practice*, 2nd Edn. London: Sage.

Lanier, J., (2011) *You are not a gadget: A manifesto*. London: Penguin Books.

Leadbeater, C., (2009) *We-think: Mass innovation, not mass production*, 2nd Edn. London: Profile Books.

Lessig, L., (2004) *Free culture: How big media uses technology and the law to lock down culture and control creativity*. New York: Penguin Press.

Marsden, S., (2017) *Positioning publishing studies in the cultural economy*. www.interscriptjournal.com/online-magazine/positioning-publishing-studies-in-the-cultural-economy (accessed 8.24.19).

McKinsey, (2019) *Generation Z characteristics and its implications for companies*. www.mckinsey.com/industries/consumer-packaged-goods/our-insights/true-gen-generation-z-and-its-implications-for-companies

McRobbie, A., (2016) *Be creative: Making a living in the new culture industries*. Chichester: John Wiley & Sons.

Naughton, J., (2012) *From Gutenberg to Zuckerberg: What you really need to know about the internet*. London: Quercus.

OC&C, (2019) *A generation without borders*. www.occstrategy.com/media/1807/a-generation-without-borders_gc.pdf

Rushkoff, D., (2011) *Life Inc*. New York: Penguin.

Ryan, B., (1992) *Making capital from culture: The corporate form of capitalist cultural production*. Berlin: de Gruyter.

Sawyer, K., (2017) *Group genius: The creative power of collaboration*. London: Hachette.

Starkey, K., Barnatt, C., Tempest, S., (2000) Beyond networks and hierarchies: Latent organizations in the U.K. television industry. *Organization Science* 11, 299–305.

Steiner, A., (2018) The global book: Micropublishing, conglomerate production, and digital market structures. *Publishing Research Quarterly* 34, 118–132. https://doi.org/10.1007/s12109-017-9558-8

Thompson, J.B., (2012) *Merchants of culture: The publishing business in the twenty-first century*, 2nd Edn. Cambridge: Polity.

Throsby, D., (2008) The concentric circles model of the cultural industries. *Cultural Trends* 17, 147–164. https://doi.org/10.1080/09548960802361951

Toffler, A., (1970) *Future shock*. New York: Random House.

Tzuo, T., Weisert, G., (2018) *Subscribed: Why the subscription model will be your company's future – and what to do about it*. New York: Penguin.

WIPO, (2015) *How to make a living in the creative industries*. wipo_pub_cr_2016_1.pdf. www.wipo.int/edocs/pubdocs/en/wipo_pub_cr_2016_1.pdf

4 Mapping collaboration theory and creative collaboration

Introduction

Collaboration is regarded as central to creative production (Graham and Gandini, 2017). As outlined in the previous chapter, the creative arena thrives on collaborative activity, and many of its structures and patterns of work are centred on this. Collaborations, of course, exist across all industries: they are specific entities that share certain characteristics in the way they form and operate. They are not, for example, outward-facing team projects, nor are they full mergers of business activities. They can be considered as strategic in outlook and ambition (Kaats and Opheij, 2014) and complex in their organisation; they can be large or small in scale, focused on products or on business activities and functions. The exact outcome is not always clear when the collaboration is centred on innovation, but the motivation for taking part usually is. Of the digital case studies presented here, three focus on developing and making innovative digital products for storytelling, education and research; the fourth is focused on the organisation, specifically how a company can create a culture of collaboration in order to help it develop new products and to refine and innovate around business functions as well as solve problems.

This chapter will explore the emergent definitions of collaborations (and related emergent collaboration theory) as well as the characteristics of collaborative activity. It will then explore the behaviours of collaborations, outlining the processes through which a collaboration moves, in order to describe the collaborations under examination here, as well as pinpoint the attributes that lead to successful collaborations.

Collaboration theory combines a variety of different disciplines; the emphasis of this chapter is on outlining a collaboration theory that is appropriate for creative environments. As a result, the chapter looks at what makes a collaboration creative, and widens that examination to assess how collaborations tend to operate in the creative industries. This lays out the central features of collaborations that will be explored in the case studies in subsequent chapters. This chapter will conclude with some detail on the Kaats and Opheij (2014) typology for collaborations, which will be used to assess how far the cases are entrepreneurial and exploratory in nature.

DOI: 10.4324/9781003378211-4

Defining 'Collaboration'

In general, the term 'collaboration' is applied loosely to several different organisational constructs such as alliances, joint ventures and strategic partnerships (and including subset domains such as 'dynamics of cooperation') all of which are tackled using different theoretical frameworks: economic, managerial, organisational, sociological. Many definitions focus on a specific behaviour within the collaboration (e.g. around decision making, problem solving or power sharing within groups).

A 'collaboration' is defined by Wood and Gray as an 'interorganisational phenomenon designed to achieve desired ends that no single organisation can achieve acting unilaterally' (1991:140). This is the underlying definition that forms the basis of this chapter. While there are other definitions, this one is useful in that it takes an organisational behaviour approach to cooperative activities between companies; implicit is the fact that the outcomes cannot be achieved by a company on its own. This recognises that the variety of different partners is key as well as the strategic importance of the activity for the wider companies involved; it also acknowledges that the collaboration sits as a separate entity. Furthermore, by looking at Wood and Gray's wider definition, the prospect of collaboration is tied to a company's aim to develop something new, reflecting a focus on innovation; a collaboration extends the opportunity of a company to achieve something original and different by working with others. It is this aspect of collaboration that becomes of interest when considering creative digital partnerships.

Therefore, this research takes the view that a collaboration is an activity that involves a number of partners that come from different organisations and/ or roles in order to work together on a specific strategic project that is beneficial to them all. This helps the research consider the collaboration from the point of view of the partners involved (and their parent organisations) and not just on the collaboration itself.

Looking for 'collaboration theory'

'Collaboration theory' is not a specific entity, though researchers in different disciplines do, on occasion, use the term. Collaboration theories essentially exist only as a range of different approaches to partnerships between two or more organisations. Various definitions emerge from the literature, as one might expect in a topic that attracts multidisciplinary approaches. For instance, there is a biological approach which arises from one evolutionary theory that survival is about cooperation (De Waal, 2006, cited in Kaats and Opheij, 2014), while the fields of psychology and mathematics explore influences of cooperative and competitive behaviour in game theory. A more defined approach to collaboration can be found in public sector studies, where much of the industry's activity is based around partnerships between private and public organisations; here, theories of collaboration follow specific rules for engagement and circumscribed sets of measures to evaluate success have developed (Gajda, 2004). But while there is specific 'collaboration' discourse for these areas, there are complaints that theories are applied almost randomly and are forced to fit whatever is being examined, to explain particular events and behaviours; this arises because the area has no overall theory, nor is a domain clearly demarcated (Bell et al., 2006; Hennart, 2006). The field is, therefore, 'fragmented, lacks coherence and has produced non-comparable research' (Hennart, 2006:1608).

Generic collaborative activity

Nevertheless, while collaboration theory may be nebulous, in order to study and assess collaborative activities, researchers have looked at ways to break down the activities and processes of a collaboration. There are various studies that focus more on the collaborative activity itself and its importance, without being specific to one industry or sector. They take a variety of angles. There are business studies approaches to the practical issues of collaboration, such as team working and group behaviour for efficient management. Collaboration also sits within a sociological discourse around sharing and connecting behaviours that lead to new ways of producing and new outputs (Davies, 2017; Gauntlett, 2011; Jenkins, 2006; Sennett, 2012). Some writers emphasise the nature of sharing, as a new style of social being is emerging due to the opportunities of the digital age; this leads into a Marxist-nuanced theory on the nature of labour, craft and happiness (Gauntlett, 2011; Hesmondhalgh and Baker, 2011; Shirky, 2008). Collaborative outputs are also examined: they might be anything from theory development within scientific collaborations (Levine and Moreland, 2004) to artistic endeavours among creative groups (Graham and Gandini, 2017; Farrell, 2003).

The emphasis of these approaches is that collaborations can lead to an understanding about creativity and innovation that does, in turn, have relevance for aspects of industrial development and opportunities for business and economic growth. It also reflects organisational behaviour literature around the stimulation of new ideas essential for economic development (Castells, 2009; Bilton, 2006; Kung, 2016; Leadbeater, 2009; Shirky, 2008). What the descriptions of generic collaborations all share, driven by organisational behaviour and project management theory, is a recognition that a collaboration stands alone with its own project-oriented ecosystem (Grabher, 2004) separate to the organisations of the constituent partners.

Defining frameworks to test collaborations

Researchers have taken different approaches to creating a methodology for understanding the behaviour of a collaboration. Some studies take a process approach to understand how and why they are formed; others track the collaboration's stages chronologically; while further studies draw out key themes that are critical to all collaborations.

One approach is to consider a definition of collaborations that centres on the sort of activity they are expected to undertake. Stakeholders have gathered to address something specific; they must share mutual expectations of goals and outcomes as well as develop temporary structures to undertake the collaboration. They are reasonably frequently instituted to deal with some sort of jointly perceived problems and so have a specific outcome in mind.

However, some collaborations, particularly in the creative area, are less about solving a particular problem and more about sharing expertise to make something new. Here the outcome of the collaboration is less clear-cut. This still might be instituted in order to solve some sort of wider issue, such as the need to compete effectively in a changing marketplace (as envisioned by Castells, 2009), or the need for a different resource base in order to develop new products which cannot be done without outside help (Kaats and Opheij, 2014). In this sense outcomes are less specific.

Several studies aim to break down the collaboration into component stages. Wood and Gray (1991) employ a simple three-stage approach which can be helpful: they divide action of the collaboration into the pre-conditions (as it were the formation stage), the process (the operation stage) and the outcomes. Each stage should have clear and distinctive characteristics that should form part of a general theory of collaboration; so that by examining how a collaboration starts, it should be easy to test then whether or not it is a collaboration (Wood and Gray, 1991).

These stages are then broken down into more specific sociological processes involved in order to identify key attributes of a collaboration. For instance, in the formation stage, Wood and Gray identify the role of the convener, the environments in which they begin to happen and the relationships between participants (1991). They believe a clear delineation of the role of the convenor is essential to the understanding of a collaboration's second stage, that of operation. Their convenor role bears similarities to the broker role in network theory (explored in Chapter 5). This breakdown of the collaboration is a useful way to examine the case studies in the research.

Kaats and Opheij (2014) adopt a similar approach, exploring the vision that leads to the project set-up. Stages of development and ongoing management are then examined, with characteristics emerging around themes such as autonomy and decision making. Finally, they recognise a variety of different outcomes which for them is critical in terms of their typology for successful partnerships. From this they develop four distinctive collaborative styles, which will be explored later in the chapter.

Features of the collaborations that flow through all these different stages are central for Daoudi and Bourgault (2012); they focus on relationships within the collaboration as an alternative way to examine them. They study collaborations in terms of issues such as the autonomy of the collaboration, how the relationships between partners work and where power resides. Certain types of managerial systems may be put in place, for instance to deal with decision making and problem solving (Olszewski, 2023); these also become part of these sorts of definitions.

Combining these different approaches leads this research to adopt the following framework for case study analysis, which takes a stage-by-stage approach while integrating the motivations and relationships that lead to the collaboration in the first place and influence its behaviour:

• Formation – how the collaborations form, including consideration of how people connect through networks, the sorts of people who convene them and the vision for the collaboration (how far is the journey important).
• Operation – this includes aspects of communication, levels of autonomy and power and processes for shared decision-making and ways to understand the organic nature of their progress.
• Outcomes – what outcomes proceed from them in terms of creative products or problem solving and how these are shared between participants.

These stages set up tangible ways in which to assess collaborations. The chronology of each collaboration can be examined, and then themes can emerge at each stage.

Creative digital collaborations

This framework is suitable for assessing many sorts of collaboration. However, the projects studied here are focused on developing new types of digital products, and there is a level of creativity at play that makes these projects stand out. Because this research examines creative collaborations, there are additional themes that emerge in relation to the nature of creativity and innovation.

Publishing, as a creative industry facing the impact of digital change, is particularly concerned with creative responses to the challenges of its business environment. Collaboration can be seen as a process that facilitates creativity (Sawyer, 2017); they are formal activities that are a part of creativity management: 'team-based innovation is an attempt to build a collective model of creativity' (Bilton, 2006:39); Graham and Gandini also note this 'managerialised emphasis' (2017:5). If innovation is at the heart of a creative collaboration, what makes the collaboration creative?

Conditions for forming creative collaborations

Innovation at one level can be about new ideas and new theories. Conditions therefore need to be ripe to lead to the initiation of new creative collaborations, particularly in relation to people and context. In an exploration of the way group collaborations can lead to innovative thinking, Levine and

Moreland (2004) examine theory development in both scientific and cultural environments; for them theory development emerges from creative thinking. They aim to identify the social context of collaborations from which creativity emerges and in doing so to look at group formation and group performance (the first two stages of Wood and Gray, 1991); they identify what leads to creative collaboration. Sawyer (2017) similarly recognises the need to create situations purposefully, where creativity flourishes, bringing many ideas together.

In terms of group formation, various characteristics emerge: Levine and Moreland (2004) identify such as a 'matchmaker' figure which is similar to Wood and Gray's convenor (1991) or the broker in network theory. These matchmakers are relatively loose roles that emerge as groups of scientific or artistic individuals (Farrell, 2003) organically link together to undertake collaborative working. While publishing collaborations, emerging as they do from business imperatives, may be more pre-planned than emergent, nevertheless it is of interest to understand how connections are made in the first place and the sorts of people pre-disposed to connect, something network theory in the next chapter can help elucidate.

There is also a 'magnet-place' where groups start to come together (Farrell, 2003), or contexts which help spark ideas (Sawyer, 2017). These are of interest, as spaces which encourage and facilitate collaboration, and which enable networks to operate effectively, are becoming key to the industry, and something this research will explore. Spaces are also central to Bilton's view of collaboration (2006); these are not always physical spaces, but the point is that some sort of 'other' space is allowed for collaboration to take place, allowing freedom to experiment.

Divergence and convergent thinking in group make-up

Group composition is important for creative thinking, as the diversity of participants is one of the drivers of the creative outcome; divergence of thinking is important, to bring a variety of minds to a project (Bilton, 2006; Sawyer, 2017; Uzzi and Spiro, 2005). Uzzi and Sprio summarise this when they say, 'we know creativity is spurred when diverse ideas are united or when creative material in one domain inspires or forces fresh thinking in another' (Uzzi and Spiro, 2005:447). For Bilton, 'creative tension' plays an important part of creativity itself and the effective management of creativity. Isaksen recognises that creativity 'involves, linked together, two or more ideas so as to produce something new and useful or something new and beautiful, or both' (Isaksen, 1987: cited in Farrell, 2003:114). So, it is important for publishers to engage a range of people with diverse backgrounds for new style creative collaborations.

But divergence on its own would not be effective without some areas of convergence (as divergence can lead to destructive behaviour and conflict). Collaboration helps to expand opportunities quickly, and friction created by the diversity in the collaboration leads to the new ideas; but some convergent thinking then takes place to focus in on one new idea to develop and test. Levine and Moreland identify 'different but complementary knowledge' (2004). Group processes lead to creative thinking in terms of idea generation, review and acceptance; an inductive process can mediate the diversity in order to reach an outcome (Leadbeater, 2009; Sawyer, 2017).

Further complex organisational problems are raised by diversity (Daoudi and Bourgault, 2012). Discontinuity exists not just between people, but between time zones, locations, work practices as well as technological and cultural differences. The collaborative dynamics around diversity can lead to problems. But discontinuity is something that not only can be overcome but also encouraged. It can be a problem for collaborations to start to work effectively, but the richness it brings can lead to good outcomes. Work practices are the biggest barrier to effective collaboration (Daoudi and Bourgault, 2012), and so attention needs to be paid to the working arrangements to ensure collaborations can operate effectively in order to encourage creativity.

Trust between partners

Themes that emerge particularly strongly in collaborations about developing new ideas and sharing or pooling knowledge are those of trust and support. Small collaborations will often have greater potential, as it is often easier to create an emotionally supportive environment (Levine and Moreland, 1994).

If the outcome is to be creative, the process of articulating ideas can help lead to a new idea (Farrell, 2003; Levine and Moreland, 2004). For publishing, each project is potentially doing something new, particularly in the digital space where there are no strict rules for what a product might look like. For this reason, the creative opportunities are very open-ended, and the products are likely to be illustrative of an open, creative discussion across different parties. The more divergent thinking, the better, but trust between partners to learn from each other and to be open to creative leaps is important. Trust is key to allow open sharing of ideas as well as the confidence to take risks (Levine and Moreland, 2004; Olszewski, 2023).

These issues of trust and credibility relate to belief in the skills of the other participants or companies; participants need to respect the expertise of their partners, as by doing so they will be able to go further with the creative ideas. In this sense successful creative collaborations need to have an equality among partners, each of whom respects the others and brings something distinct to the table. As Farrell says, partners 'are likely to be roughly similar in their levels of expertise in their discipline . . . they have relatively equal status and relatively equal resources (2003:19–20). This allows for effective exchange and sharing, a central axis for Kaats and Opheij's model of strategic partnership. Potential for conflict can still arise where the balance may be disrupted by other processes in the collaboration, for instance on aspects of ownership of the outcome (if it is a product, for instance) or levels of risk taking.

Risk for creative projects

Creativity involves elements of risk, particularly in relation to the economic outcomes for the creative industries (Uzzi and Spiro, 2005). Experimentation means taking risks, and the creative aspects of the collaborative activity of Levine and Moreland (2004) or Farrell (2003) illustrate the need to push boundaries. However, in certain creative industries, an overriding issue is that outcomes must be commercial as well as critically acclaimed when measuring success. This can add a variable for assessing creativity; because of the commercial demands, there is an added friction when trying to be creative. The question of balance emerges again: publishing collaborations can be creative, but they need to ensure they follow certain conventions in order to be commercially viable. The play of divergent and convergent thinking within a collaboration is important. When developing something innovative or experimental, there needs to be a subtle understanding among partners of exactly how much risk they are happy to take in terms of commercial imperatives. The project ecology needs to embody this recognition of risk in the way it works so that decision making is effective (Grabher, 2004).

Vision development and collaboration outcomes

One area of collaboration activity that is less well explored is that of vision development. Yet it is an important way to plan for accepted levels of risk as, in project management theory, setting clear goals is an essential and early stage of the project. Collaboration research may veer away from exploring vision development as theorists tend to focus on unpicking abstract aspects of collaborations (e.g. distribution of power) rather than dealing with pre-defined outcomes. Nevertheless, given the way creative projects need actively to negotiate a balance between creative and commercial risk, the vision becomes central to effective collaboration. Kaats and Opheij (2014) recognise that the outcome of a partnership is part of its defining characteristics: having some sort of vision, even if it is a fairly open one (e.g. that some sort of digital project will emerge), is necessary in order to ensure the collaboration is effective. They give weight to the importance of shared goals in collaborative work, building on themes around relationships and trust.

Further, they highlight the importance of value. The collaboration creates value for partners – this may be different for different participants but nevertheless must be clearly present and measurable in some way. The quality of the outcome, the creative response, the solution to problems or the learning may all be part of the value of a project. As Osborn and Hagedoorn suggest, the immediate returns of a collaboration are not as critical a gain as the 'building of technical capability, tacit knowledge or understanding of rapidly changing market' (1997:270).

The initial vision may be kindled by the broker, while the subsequent evolution of that vision then becomes important for the process of the collaboration.

The vision needs to be clear enough to ensure all participants engage with it, yet feel flexible enough that it can be change or adapted where necessary (in order to allow for creative leaps) (Olszewski, 2023). Ownership of that vision needs, therefore, to be shared equally so all participants feel they can work with it.

Formal and informal processes of management

As a collaboration gets going, specific project behaviours are noted to be key to successful outcomes. While Levine and Moreland note that a process towards theory development emerges in the behaviour of a collaboration, around how ideas are put forward and assessed, this process is not overt but emerges as the collaboration evolves. Sawyer also identifies a pattern of behaviours that can help a collaboration, typifying this more as a form of improvisation (2017). While formal project management techniques can be deployed, a level of informality may also be apparent (Kaats and Opheij, 2014) due to the closeness of partners. Linked to this is a level of autonomy, whereby members of the collaboration have the authority to make decisions without necessarily referring back to the parent organisation, allowing for a level of agility; this draws on the level of expertise of the main leaders of the collaboration, while reflecting trust not just within the collaboration but back to the parent organisation. Informality here can help support creativity and disruptive thinking (Olszewski, 2023).

So, theories of collaboration, particularly when applied to creative projects within creative industries, reveal some particular attributes that may be studied in the publishing collaborations case studies. These areas of focus are:

- The role of the broker (or convenor) who helps form a collaboration
- The importance of divergent thinking for creativity
- Trust in order to make creative leaps
- Attitudes to risk when trying new things, balanced with commercial necessity
- The evolution of shared visions that allow for a level of flexibility and creativity
- Formality and informality of styles of operation

From each of these themes it has been seen that the matter of balance is central. For publishing collaborations, this balance is at the heart of the ability to be innovative while also commercially strategic (Bérubé and Gauthier, 2023).

Strategic collaboration

Now that we have examined attributes that make collaboration work effectively, and explored how a collaboration can manifest creativity in particular, it is important to focus also on the strategic imperative of undertaking collaborations for the wider company. Business, economics and corporate strategy studies see collaborations as providing ways to tackle systemic issues in growing markets or industries (Kaats and Opheij, 2014; Sawyer, 2017). Organisations can be set up to facilitate collaborations in order to further the strategic aims of a business. Publishing is under pressure from digital transformation and challenges to their structure and workflow. The digital collaborations studied in this research are focused on digital innovation partly because of the need for publishers to strategise around their digital future. These projects are not numerous, but they are some of the more innovative projects publishers are undertaking as they try to experiment in digital formats. Organisations want to understand how to facilitate effective collaborations that will lead to successful innovation.

Categories of strategic collaboration

If collaboration is one of the ways for an organisation to be more experimental, the typology laid out by Kaats and Opheij (2014) is helpful as a way to identify the collaborations that are more creative and strategic in this way. They analyse the nature of different business collaborations in terms of what the collaboration is trying to achieve. By providing a categorisation for different collaborations, along with variables that can be explored for each type, the model Kaats and Opheji develop helps assess the different emphases of collaborations depending on their aims, structure and behaviour. These facets dovetail with the characteristics already highlighted around the way collaborations are set up and the processes they use once in motion.

Kaats and Opheij present four different types of collaborative activity: transactional, functional, exploratory and entrepreneurial. Of these four, there is a link between transactional and functional: they reflect more traditional collaborative styles that generally involve working with existing business contacts and suppliers. They also integrate collaborative activity in a more normative way to the business and focus on specifics such as refining a supply chain or outsourcing a particular activity from the main business.

On the other hand, explorative and entrepreneurial collaborations can be regarded as newer in approach for certain sectors which are not necessarily accustomed to behaving in this way: firms that typically deal with innovation and experimentation as part of the modus operandi of their business may be more accustomed to these models. Kaats and Opheij do not necessarily see any collaborative type as more or less important than another; that depends on the company strategy. But they do make the point that increasingly complex managerial situations are leading to the fact collaborations no longer 'fit inside the box: they are increasingly region, sector or discipline transcending' (2014:11). In particular the explorative and entrepreneurial approaches reflect the need for more innovation-based models to compete in a more complex business environment. As they unpick the characteristics of these four types of collaboration, they make a clear link between these latter two types on this basis.

Exploratory and entrepreneurial models

Kaats and Opheij (2014) overlay on Marco de Witte and colleagues' model of change (2012) where the first type (or order) of change focuses on improving the business, the second is about transforming and the third involves systemic change in terms of transition. Certain types of collaboration can help transform and transition (Olszewski, 2023).

For publishing, the changing competitive environment requires stretching business models and developing new projects as they transition to managing in a new climate. There is an implication that while all collaborations involve some level of managing complexity and mutual problem solving, it is the explorative and entrepreneurial collaborations that are more appropriate; they are important where business environments are changing rapidly, dealing with 'catalytic themes' (2014:25). These types of collaboration promote 'invention and development', and outcomes are directed at 'penetrating new markets, developing new products or technologies' (2014:26) where to try to do so alone would be impossible: 'no organisation can survive alone, nor can any one organisation single-handedly solve the complex issues of our day' (2014:89), building on themes raised by Manuel Castells (2009). Osborn and Hagedoorn also highlight this issue: 'numerous studies suggest the use of alliances has been more common in areas in which firms face daunting technological challenge' (1997:269). Kaats and Opheij particularly focus on new business models suggesting that there is a current need to explore alternative ways of dealing with the changing business environment: they draw interesting connections between the need to have access to, rather than own, resources; so collaboration leads to greater trust, sharing and the ability to connect. All themes that emerge in wider observations about the changing economy are outlined by writers such as Castells (2009) or Rifkin (2014).

The transactional and functional types of collaboration may be more inter-organisational, where partnerships are already established, while the explorative and entrepreneurial routes evolve and may lead to new and unexpected outcomes. There is no particular hierarchy in the minds of Kaats and Opheij (2014) as they see all these collaborative activities as relevant and context dependent: it is by understanding the type of collaboration that you are in that you can ensure the effective measures to model success are in place. The importance for this research is that the second two types represent less traditional types of collaboration for publishing and yet seem to be on the increase.

The entrepreneurial and explorative models also reflect an approach to disruptive innovation where unpredictable changes within the market are at the core of the drive for innovation (Kung, 2008:138). The danger is that incumbents may disregard disruptive innovation in favour of continuous improvement of existing products; by doing this they do not have to make structural changes, but they then may not change their architecture quickly enough to respond to the shift in markets. This has resonance with the legacy issues publishers face, for instance. For Kaats and Opheij (2014), explorative and entrepreneurial collaborations are a way to counter this: they allow ways to experiment in response to the changing marketplace without disrupting normal business while the experimentation is happening; and collaboration itself reflects the organisation's agility to accommodate new structures in which to experiment, without reorganising its core business too early. Kaats and Opheij note that organisations are 'experimenting intensively with organisational forms that offer more room for variety and flexibility' (2014:76), noting that the challenges these organisations face are in a continuous state of flux, so it is desirable to remain alert and react fast. For publishing the digital challenges, as seen previously, are such that collaborative activity can be a way to respond to try new things and test the waters, while remaining flexible and nimble. Kaats and Opheij additionally comment that organisations need to build more of a culture of collaborative activity; companies need to institute ways to manage collaborations in order to be able to keep trying new projects with new partners (2014:9).

Conclusion – the research proposition and framework for exploring the cases

While this chapter has looked at collaboration from a variety of angles, similar themes have emerged from the various theoretical approaches examined around issues of creativity, trust, risk and process. From this we can see that collaborations are different from other forms of partnerships. They carry specific features that reflect their uniqueness as an organisational response to challenging environments. This research proposes that entrepreneurial and exploratory styles of collaborations are required for publishers to be innovative in arenas where experimentation is required. 'Traditional' publishing structures have built-in limitations indicating that creative digital new product development may not be fully supported. By taking a collaborative approach, publishers can generate new ideas and strategies for creative digital projects. Collaborations can contain a different balance of creative and commercial imperatives, of risk and stability, without impacting the main publishing company's model.

The research uses the typology laid out by Kaats and Opheij to test how far these digital collaborations fit either the entrepreneurial or exploratory models (as opposed to the transactional and functional models). The research will break down the collaborations into stages: formation, operation and outcomes. The characteristics that have emerged, particularly those that instil creativity, will be examined in these three stages, paying particular attention to the characteristics of creative industries, in order to assess ways in which collaboration can be effective. It should be possible to conclude how far these projects are successful at achieving their goals for creativity and innovation, and to identify the features that are key to this success as well as understand what sorts of structures need to be in place to ensure that creative collaborations like these can flourish. It is likely that contradictions will emerge; as Osborn and Hagedoorn say, collaborations 'are temporary mechanisms and long-lasting relationships. They are cooperative and competitive weapons. Each is unique but they often share similar properties. They have intended purposes yet their emergent benefits may be more important' (1997:274). The dualities set up by Osborn and Hagedoorn appear to reflect the challenges of effective explorative and entrepreneurial collaborations outlined by Kaats and Opheij. Balances are required to ensure commercial and creative innovation is achieved, while understanding how to set up effective collaborations may lead to a useful structural response to digital change.

References

Bell, J., den Ouden, B., Ziggers, G.W., (2006) Dynamics of cooperation: At the brink of irrelevance. *Journal of Management Studies* 43, 1607–1619. https://doi.org/10.1111/j.1467-6486.2006.00653.x

Bérubé, J., Gauthier, J.-B., (2023) Managing projects in creative industries: A compromise between artistic and project management values. *Creative Industries Journal* 16, 76–95. https://doi.org/10.1080/17510694.2021.197 9278

Bilton, C., (2006) *Management and creativity: From creative industries to creative management.* Chichester: John Wiley & Sons.

Castells, M., (2009) *The rise of the network society: Information age: Economy, society, and culture,* 2nd Edn. Chichester: Wiley-Blackwell.

Daoudi, J., Bourgault, M., (2012) Discontinuity and collaboration: Theory and evidence from technological projects. *International Journal of Innovation Management* 16, 1. https://doi.org/10.1142/S1363919612400129

Davies, R., (2017) Collaborative production and the transformation of publishing, in: Graham J., Gandini A. (Eds.) *Collaborative Production in the Creative Industries.* London: Westminster University Press, pp. 51–67. https://doi.org/10.16997/book4.d

de Waal, F., (2006) *Our inner ape: A leading primatologist explains why we are who we are.* New York: Riverhead Books.

de Witte, M., Jonker, J., Vink, M., (2012) *Essences of management of change.* Deventer: Kluwer.

Farrell, M.P., (2003) *Collaborative circles: Friendship dynamics and creative work.* Chicago: University of Chicago Press.

Gajda, R., (2004) Utilizing collaboration theory to evaluate strategic alliances. *American Journal of Evaluation* 25, 65–77. https://doi.org/10.1177/109821400402500105

Gauntlett, D., (2011) *Making is connecting: The social meaning of creativity, from DIY and knitting to YouTube and Web 2.0.* Cambridge: Polity.

Grabher, G., (2004) Learning in projects, remembering in networks? Communality, sociality, and connectivity in project ecologies. *European Urban and Regional Studies* 11, 103–123. https://doi.org/10.1177/0969776404041417

Graham, J., Gandini, A., (2017) Introduction: Collaborative production in the creative industries, in: Graham J., Gandini A. (Eds.), *Collaborative production in the creative industries*, London: Westminster University Press, pp. 1–14. https://doi.org/10.16997/book4.a

Hennart, J.-F., (2006) Alliance research: Less is more. *Journal of Management Studies* 43, 1621–1628. https://doi.org/10.1111/j.1467-6486.2006.00654.x

Hesmondhalgh, D., Baker, S., (2011) *Creative labour: Media work in three cultural industries.* London: Routledge.

Isaksen, S., (1987), *Frontiers of Creativity Reseasrch.* Buffalo: Bearly Limited.

Jenkins, H., (2006) *Convergence culture: Where old and new media collide.* New York: NYU Press.

Kaats, E., Opheij, W., (2014) *Creating conditions for promising collaboration: Alliances, networks, chains, strategic partnerships.* New York: Springer.

Kung, L., (2008) *Strategic management in the media.* London: Sage.

Kung, L., (2016) *Strategic management in the media: Theory to practice*, 2nd Edn. London: Sage.

Leadbeater, C., (2009) *We-think: Mass innovation, not mass production.* London: Profile Books.

Levine, J.M., Moreland, R.L., (2004) Collaboration: The social context of theory development. *Personality and Social Psychology Review* 8, 164–172. https://doi.org/10.1207/s15327957pspr0802_10

Olszewski, M., (2023) Agile project management as a stage for creativity: A conceptual framework of five creativity-conducive spaces. *International Journal of Managing Projects in Business* 16, 496–520. https://doi.org/10.1108/IJMPB-05-2022-0111

Osborn, R.N., Hagedoorn, J., (1997) The institutionalization and evolutionary dynamics of interorganizational alliances and networks. *Academy of Management Journal* 40, 261–278. https://doi.org/10.2307/256883

Rifkin, J., (2014) *The zero marginal cost society: The internet of things, the collaborative commons, and the eclipse of capitalism.* New York: Palgrave Macmillan.

Sawyer, K., (2017) *Group genius: The creative power of collaboration.* London: Hachette.

Sennett, R., (2012) *Together: The rituals, pleasures and politics of cooperation.* London: Penguin.

Shirky, C., (2008) *Here comes everybody: The power of organizing without organizations.* New York: Penguin Press.

Uzzi, B., Spiro, J., (2005) Collaboration and creativity: The small world problem. *American Journal of Sociology* 111, 447–504. https://doi.org/10.1086/432782

Wood, D.J., Gray, B., (1991) Toward a comprehensive theory of collaboration. *Journal of Applied Behavioral Science* 27, 139–162. https://doi.org/10.1177/0021886391272001

5   Network theory, creative industries and publishing

Introduction

Successful innovation is driven by new ideas and new approaches – collaboration helps bring new ideas to fruition – but how do people make the connections in the first place? If collaborative activity is an effective way to experiment and innovate, (Bilton, 2006) and to develop strategic alliances (Kung, 2008), networks are required to create these collaborative opportunities. As organisational structures move from 'stable arrangements to increasingly fluid ones' (Kung, 2008:193), the network becomes more important as a way to facilitate effective project-based business activity and manage strategic growth. While publishing shares characteristics with the wider sector, it still needs to make connections and develop new relationships; developing the creative network is key to this.

Networks in publishing exist at a formal level. The Independent Alliance in the UK, for instance, involving among others Faber and Faber, Canongate and Pushkin Press, reflect this sort of way of working, where certain resources can be pooled to achieve critical mass for particular functions, while individual firms retain autonomy and independence. At a more informal level, in-house publishing staff will have networks of freelancers and suppliers to take on regular work such as copy editing or typesetting (Heebels et al., 2013). However, networks do more than this: they hold in them the *potential* to be creative. Networks enable an organisation to mix and change creative environments and to connect in new ways to spark novel ideas. If networks are developed and used effectively, in entrepreneurial ways, this should allow for a more sustainable approach to innovation (Bilton, 2006).

Networks are particularly important at the formation stage of collaborations as new partners are sought. Connections made between participants can themselves inspire new collaborative activity. Networks then continue to play a part as projects develop: new people join the collaboration to help solve problems, and new ideas continue to emerge as the project progresses. The strength of the network to continue to operate effectively, after the project is over, is also a consideration, as it can then lead to the next collaboration.

DOI: 10.4324/9781003378211-5

This chapter first briefly outlines the mechanics of the way networks work, as applied to creative business practice. Outlining well-established terminology of strong and weak ties, and structural holes, it examines their application in a creative industries arena. It then illustrates how the creative industries are structured around network activity together with aspects of value in networks. From that it then draws out the key aspects that will be examined in the research of the cases.

How networks work and their application to the creative sector

Discussions on networks can encompass many topics, including digital connectivity, convergence cultures, hyper textuality and new media ecosystems (Scolari, 2019). However, when examining management practices and collaborative activity, the study of networks centres on connections between people and how those relationships work. While network theory is studied across all sorts of business activity, many of the academic studies are situated in creative industries; this is because of the high occurrence of projects that depend on networks for their development and execution, and so the environment for networks is particularly active in this arena (Borgatti and Lopez-Kidwell, 2011; Burt, 2004; Grabher, 2004a; Graham and Gandini, 2017; Granovetter, 1973). Creativity is 'a distributed and embedded cultural process' (Daskalaki, 2010:1650). As such, network behaviour can enhance creative activity: as Graham and Gandini state: 'individual action in a networked context has become integral to the enactment of creative work' (2017:6). Comparative studies are particularly interesting as they reveal the way businesses in the creative sector operate differently from other types of industry, for instance, in nurturing creativity (Grabher, 2004a, 2004b).

Connections within networks – strong and weak ties

Networks are formed out of a variety of ties reflecting an individual's connection with someone else (Bilton, 2006; Borgatti and Lopez-Kidwell, 2011; Granovetter, 1973; Heebels et al., 2013). These ties can cluster and sit within, and external to, organisations. Individuals will naturally have many ties of different sorts: some will be more formal, maybe due to their job function or position in an organisational structure; others will be informal, where they connect with others perhaps on more social terms. These do not always have to be personal ties of friendship, but they are social ties nevertheless. They may be typified in different ways, such as advice networks or friendship networks. These become particularly important for project-based industries.

These ties can be defined as strong or weak depending on a variety of variables (Borgatti and Lopez-Kidwell, 2011; Grabher, 2004a, 2004b;

Granovetter, 1973), such as emotional intensity or time. Creative industries tend to be characterised by reasonably complex ties, often referred to as multiplexity of ties; this means combinations of ties, both different sorts of relationships with different people, and different relationships with the same person (Parker, 2004). Weak ties reflect a very loose link between network clusters; it may be only one person makes the link. Where that link is made, however, it can be quite critical to aspects of innovation; innovative thinking can benefit from diversity, as a variety of different sorts of people connect and so develop new directions. This relates to diffusion theory: a weak link helps an idea spread further so as to reach 'a larger number of people and traverse greater social distance when passed through weak ties' (Granovetter, 1973:1366). This is the nub of the spread of ideas, and this leads to creativity. Strong ties mean the ideas spread around and around the same group so they never get onto the margins to make the leap. For Bilton, the 'transitions' between the ties, particularly those at the periphery of the network, are where creativity resides (2006:48).

Balance of network ties in publishing

Barbara Heebels et al. (2013) look at the publishing industry, exploring network connections using these theories (in particular Grabher's theories of network types, 2004a and b). They examine how the different actors work within the value chain of books. So, for publishing, the author might be connected to the industry by a weak tie, while the internal activities of the publisher, with their related network of professional suppliers, would reflect a strong tie. They break down the various relationships between different functions in order to assess how they work with their networks. There is an overarching point that the house operates as a network on different levels. Different roles in publishing houses will act in different ways when connecting, depending on the function: having an author who has worked with the publisher before already requires a more embedded approach with strong ties, working with someone closely and understanding modes of operation; but acquiring new authors needs an element of sales, and an outward connection to establish new contacts, so more open networks come into play.

   In this way any individual within a publishing house may be operating networks in a variety of ways, although some may have greater multiplexity of strong and weak ties. For Heebels et al. (2013), it is clear there is a strategic combination of these different network styles. Balancing professional and personal is critical for the publishing house negotiating the balance between its creative and commercial working. Heebels et al. say the 'tension between culture and commerce is dealt with by switching between roles' (2013:715). What they show is that there are many established network behaviours already in place in publishing so that it operates smoothly. These behaviours are almost structural in that the organisation is designed around these networks by functions: desk editorial departments, for instance, will have well-established networks with their freelancers; commissioning editors will have a looser network of external advisors. But these are all still reasonably strong, well-established ties. The broader point for publishing is that it may need to take an explicit approach to developing more outward-facing, looser networks in order to be innovative enough in a changing digital environment; this might require recognising the limitations of the existing structures which are designed more around embedded networks with strong ties.

Embeddedness and its dangers

The concept of embeddedness is a complementary theoretical framework for the issues of projects and networks introduced earlier. Embeddedness emerged as an economic theme that examined the way markets operated historically, but it makes use of network theory to examine this more closely in terms of organisational behaviours for particular sectors (Uzzi, 1997). Embedded networks are more enduring and established, operate with 'clearly defined standards of behaviour easily policed by the quick spread of information' (Granovetter, 1985:492) and are based on strong, enduring social relations – in other words, strong ties. They provide a stability to risk taking as well, which is key; and has some links to the latent organisation identified by Starkey et al. (2000), whereby new TV projects can quickly form as they are based broadly on similar people, activities and structures each time.

Embeddedness allows for more enduring relationships that mean people understand each other's ways of operation. This is important for projects, as it can provide security in a level of predictability; they are easily sustainable, and they can avoid conflict and self-interest because they have trust, which means they can combine to compete effectively if needed as well as support each other if needed (Daskalaki, 2010; Uzzi, 1997). These are all characteristics that certain aspects of publishing would recognise as important for effective project-working.

However, embeddedness can lead to problems. Starkey et al. note that latent organisations can have a lack of creativity as they operate continuously in the same way (2000); so while they are a way to manage risk, conversely, they may also be a way to dampen risk taking. There is the potential for embedded networks to operate in a limited way, even while it benefits from the security it can provide (Uzzi, 1997). Innovativeness can be hindered by working with a very embedded network, which, as Uzzi admits, can lead to sterility. However, his proposition is that, ideally, 'embedded ties enrich the network while arms-length ties prevent complete insulation of the network from market demands and possibilities' (Uzzi, 1997:59). There is a balance to be struck between a network that operates along lines that are well established, allowing for trust and mutual risk taking, and a network made up of looser ties that can be more entrepreneurial. Through new types of collaboration, publishers may be attempting to negotiate this balance. They face the challenge of not disrupting their existing business too much (embeddedness helps them function efficiently and manage risk), while introducing new ideas and ways to experiment. They may need to move beyond traditional networks to reach new creative partners. These challenges can be spotted in the case studies that are explored in later chapters.

Structural holes where creativity resides

One further framework from network theory that is useful to consider in relation to the publishing industry is that of structural holes. This concept as presented by Burt (2004) represents a way to conceptualise one route to the development of new ideas. It looks at the holes or gaps within networks. A strong network has knowledge and information which can be useful for developing innovative ideas if it can be shared more widely. Gaps exist between different strong networks which, if connected, can lead to further experimentation and innovation. Collins (1998) describes places in a network where friction leads to transfer of ideas and suggests that networks with varieties of people provide more of these friction places where creative things can happen. Here creativity is not about the individual genius but a collaborative experience: as Burt says (and as is embodied by the network), 'creativity as an import-export business' (Burt, 2004:388). This highlights the need for network exchange, across structural holes, to engender creativity though collaborative means.

These theories are in line with Granovetter, who identifies weak ties as effective for spreading ideas (1973): interesting links are made through unexpected connections, and ideas are distributed further, not recirculated around the same people. However, Burt knowledge takes this further, as he sees value in the gaps themselves (2004). For Fortou (cited in Burt), 'le vide' – or emptiness – is an important part of the drive to the formation of new ideas, operating in its way like a vacuum, or a gap that requires filling, with or without ideas. These structural holes can be organisationally important: they are 'disconnections' (Burt, 2004:388) or gaps between clusters within an organisational structure, where value may be buried, and which may reflect entrepreneurial opportunities. An individual network can have structural holes, but Burt considers the network of a wider business organisation; this contains a variety of clusters, each its own network, and between clusters too there can be structural holes.

This leads to two important considerations for a publishing company where it is seeking to be creative: first, that networks are as important inside the company as outside for creative opportunity; and second, that there are particular individuals that may well be important in developing these sorts of creative networks. Implicit in Burt's discussion is the flexibility required in an organisation to allow these structural holes to be spanned. Rigid organisations do not allow crossing and integration as easily. New connections lead to diversity, which in turn leads to new ways to solve problems and the development of new ideas; people connected across groups are 'more familiar with alternative ways of thinking and behaving, which gives them more options to select from and synthesise' (Burt, 2004:349). But this also highlights a potential problem for publishing: in developing its hierarchies and value chain so successfully and so tightly, it may have lost some of the opportunities to be creative in new ways.

Bonds and brokers – how to connect networks in creative industries

Individuals who can connect these different networks are in a strong position and can gain comparative advantages. In idea generation, someone is 'moving knowledge from this group to that' (Burt, 2004:356); the people who create bridges enable the value to be extracted from structural holes. They are needed to make the creative leaps for ideas, as they can identify opportunities and cross boundaries. Burt cites research into a variety of examples of people and institutions bridging networks, from Cosimo de Medici to IDEO product design consultants. These people could be regarded as traditional brokers, much as a literary agent might connect an author and a publisher; detailed knowledge of the existing industry is of key benefit to those brokers (Bilton, 2006). However, network theory sees more subtle versions of this. Those at the edges of networks may have links to other networks, even where their knowledge is less detailed, and so make unexpected connections between networks that are very different, linking different expertise, knowledge and mindsets.

Brokers in this sense are the people who exhibit a particular network behaviour, which enables unusual connections to be made and brings together the diversity of people that is needed in a creative collaboration (Bilton, 2006). The person who forms the collaboration brokers the relationships at the start, and holds a particular and vital role in setting projects in motion. The broker acts like a mediator within the company, the go-between who allows new partners to develop levels of trust quickly (Heebels et al., 2013; Uzzi, 1997). These brokers are important, as they sit near structural holes and so are, almost automatically, at 'higher risk of having good ideas since they enjoy more opportunities to select and synthesize alternative ways of thinking' (DeFillippi et al., 2007:512).

Understanding the nature of the network and the way knowledge spreads has significance for leadership: a leader may not be a broker, but should nevertheless be someone who can share more, connect more and mediate knowledge across a web of networks (Adams et al., 2014; Corbett and Spinello, 2020), creating situations for new ideas to be explored and to flourish.

Creative organisations and network behaviour

While network theory indicates how different network structures lead to different levels of creativity and knowledge exchange, in practical terms networks are central to the activity of many creative businesses; creative projects already reflect complex network behaviour (Davies and Sigthorsson, 2013; Hesmondhalgh, 2013). By understanding how networks operate in the sector, this research aims to explore how networks can be exploited in such a way as to lead to the most effective and creative collaborative activity.

Networks and project-based working

Creative organisations are project-centred and so, in terms of network process, certain characteristics emerge. Andreas Wittel (2001) points out that media industries are often best understood by looking at their network behaviour, particularly in a digital environment; for media practitioners, 'social relationships and networking are crucial tools and resources for a successful business' (2001:54). Wittel characterises cultural industries as ones where project-based working leads to non-linear biographies for those participating; portfolio careers and mixing and matching jobs around projects are traditionally part of the creative worker's career trajectory (Flew, 2013; Hesmondhalgh and Baker, 2011). The need to develop networks that allow creative individuals to freelance in different ways, find the next project and collaborate on different things is key to their ability to build a successful career (Davies and Sigthorsson, 2013:77); creatives need to establish their own value in their social capital (Wittel, 2001).

Networks are not just about creative individuals. They are also embedded within creative businesses. Their centrality is reflected in two important ways. The first is the persistent ties people form with each other through 'repeated organisation' around projects; the second is the way creative freelancers organise themselves through 'semi-permanent work arrangements' (Daskalaki, 2010:1650). This regularity, whereby repeated connections are made within the network, is important for getting projects going quickly or slotting freelance individuals into existing workflows efficiently. Established networks are therefore central to a creative business-like publishing, whether for drawing on a network of regular readers or using semi-permanent teams of freelance editors or project managers. This leads to certain behaviours: for example, Davies and Sigthorsson identify the need to learn collaborative skills effectively for the sort of 'high-speed collective working' (2013:99). The need to develop a collective purpose quickly, when projects are continuously forming, is key.

A further feature of the network behaviour that characterises the creative sector is that, in order for the projects to operate effectively, there needs to be some level of trust between parties, and networks need to embody that. Networks 'create sense of community and shared culture' (Davies and Sigthorsson, 2013:101; McKinlay and Smith, 2009) which makes it possible to operate even in a project-based industry. Davies and Sigthorssen see the style of working as one of 'negotiation rather than command and control' (2013:100), because each person has their own area of creative expertise and is used to working in a project-based way; roles are defined by the project and not by the hierarchies of a traditional organisation. Berube and Gauthier (2023) indicate that negotiation is key to managing the tension between artistic and project management values.

Starkey et al. (2000) describe the concept of a latent organisation that can emerge as needed, following certain norms that operate with a shared understanding of the value chain of TV programme making. This then affects the behaviour of the network which encompasses particular characteristics that, in their view, surpass network behaviour. For them, the 'latent organisation' is an organisational construct different from other network forms; similarly, Bilton describes the construction of a 'virtual organisation' (2008:128). In terms of network process, people can connect rapidly along tried and tested lines so in effect work as 'collaborations . . . kept on a low flame' (Wittel, 2001:56). Uzzi and Spiro identify the way the networks are based on shared knowledge that exists due to the constant 'configuration and reconfiguration' (2005:3) of the same participants in an enduring network.

Therefore, a balance between loose and strong networks is required: a network has to be flexible enough to allow new projects to form with different ranges of partners, while maintaining some structures that make it quick and easy for them to operate once formed. This would be familiar to certain aspects of publishing, where the need to move quickly in the production of a book means that it is useful to draw together teams of freelancers who do not require a lot of briefing because they already understand the processes of the larger organisation and of each other; continuity with the organisation and with each other exists, even though they do not work within the organisation but are employed project by project.

Project ecologies

While network processes are needed to set up each new project, Gernot Grabher has looked at the way a project itself works (2004a, 2004b) once running. He typifies projects that are from creative industries as being involving 'turbulence, ambiguity' (2004b:1500). The characteristic of 'improvising' (using jazz as a metaphor that is also adopted by Sawyer, 2017) is something he identifies in creative industries that has 'prototype organisations designed to maximise innovation' (2004b:1500). As he compares the IT industry with creative industries (both of which innovate), he focuses in on the issue of originality. For the advertising industry, a continuous change in teams, an element of ephemerality and deliberate changing of collaborative partners help ensure creativity and freshness (Grabher, 2004a, 2004b); the value of originality is also explored by Bérubé and Gauthier, 2023, as they too examine the advertising industry. Creative collaborations need to use wide networks to ensure they bring fresh new ideas forward.

As projects have their own ecology, the networks for different sorts of projects need to reflect different nuances. Publishing may be very effective at a certain type of creativity (e.g. around authors and production), but may be less creative in terms of experimenting around digital formats. It may use well-established networks and not develop new ones as effectively. Projects that are set up to help them develop more experimental digital products need to encompass networks and project ecologies that lead to creative thinking. This becomes interesting to observe in the collaborations of this study: when projects are forming, how much are the well-honed networks already in place exploited, and how much are newer network connections used? If publishers need to, and are, looking for a wider range of partners, they may need to develop newer, possibly more fragile, networks when looking outward for more collaborators. This has implications for trust and shared narratives noted earlier, but can lead to creativity. The way the collaborations operate once underway, their networked project ecology also plays a part: network sociality 'is created on a project by project basis, by the movement of ideas, the establishment of only every temporary standards and protocols. . . . [They are] open structure, able to expand almost without limits and they are highly dynamic' (Wittel, 2001:52).

Challenges of network working

There are downsides to project behaviours, as Starkey et al. (2000) point out in relation to the TV projects they studied: the network needs to have a significant volume of transactions (i.e. be kept active, connections kept alive) to ensure they remain viable. While networks involve some cushion to help manage risk, if networks are not used, they become weaker. There is also risk involved in continuous re-forming around projects, as doing so can feel more unstable compared to the persistent and secure structure of a permanent organisation. In addition, the issues around speed of response as projects have to be put in place is still a problem. As digital transformation continues, creative companies need to respond quickly.

Sennett (2012) also considers the problems in this sort of project-oriented network behaviour: the longevity of relationships is lost, and a shared narrative and value in experience are also casualties. Skills are continuously transferred and so lost to organisations from which they have moved. On the other hand, Grabher (2004a) sees danger in the longer-term network where networks that are very established and repetitive, while reducing risk, can hinder creativity. Participants have to be good at moving on, realising a partnership may be effective for only a certain amount of time. Further, projects may fail; not all experiments are successful, so participants have to let projects go. A creative network therefore is key for finding the next partner.

For publishing, there is a danger that some networks do not get renewed, but rather end up embedded so that the same group of freelancers are continuously used and new ideas do not always emerge so easily. Publishers must look for the balance between the two that achieves 'creative compatibility' (Daskalaki, 2010:1652). Their networks must remain flexible, combined and recombining, alongside the project itself, to ensure they can operate effectively. Organisations must be agile, therefore, to be able to accommodate change as projects progress.

Value in networks

Networks behave in particular ways within the creative industry, and that in itself has value. This value can exist in a network in a variety of different ways; it can lie in its latent possibility to be creative from the connections that can be made or in the diversity the network encompasses. Its value can be reflected in the skills it contains and in its ability to find knowledge from elsewhere. The act of connecting itself inspires creativity, which also has a potential value. This extends to concepts of symbolic value (Heebels et al., 2013; Thompson, 2012) which rest within the reputation of the company and its potential to be innovative in signing up exciting and important new authors and so attracting readers.

Learning, knowledge and value from networks

One of the key aspects of the value in a network is the learning that is embedded in it (Uzzi, 1997:54). For Grabher, strong, well-established networks lead to strength in 'long term collaboration with a relatively stable set of suppliers . . . [which] affords interactive learning processes' (2004b:1500). He recognises different learning styles between different industries. While some industries focus on iterative learning, accumulating knowledge progressively, for creative environments learning is a more stilted, experimental affair; creativity is provoked by sudden changes, switching around to see what works and learn new things.

The learning is important for an organisation despite the transitory nature of projects, as experience and skills are retained in some way. Network behaviour enables learning both in connecting to other people who have knowledge to bring to a project and in learning from them during the project; that learning then needs to be kept accessible, and the network can embody that, holding knowledge that can be accessed as needed. Similarly, for Daskalaki, the network itself holds that value, retaining the knowledge within the network, through keeping the connections alive (2010). Social capital is, in this way, embedded in networks, and it is due to the fact that knowledge is held in them that their power is recognised (Scolari, 2019).

Cooperation and trust through networks

For a sector that is used to taking risks around new products, networking also provides support. For industries where risk taking and experimentation are central, the network becomes something that is a point of stability in an environment that is changing rapidly and which faces fierce external competition (Wittel, 2001). Publishing straddles both internal and external project-based working; both those within a publishing company and those working as free-lancers around it will recognise that using networks is central to their activity, as it allows them to work in a project-based way. What they may not neces-sarily recognise is how far these characteristics of networks (i.e. where trust is embedded, where there is no overt central control, etc.) enable both creativity and speed of operation. These networks potentially become more important as the industry faces new risks and needs to depend on partners to innovate in ways that help them move forward.

Conclusion – the link to collaboration

Networks are central to the operation of the creative industries and in them-selves can embody creativity and opportunities to experiment. For Bell et al. (2006), network behaviour is essential to the definition of a collaboration, as each one will be formed of different people, operating in different ways. There is a dynamic at play, similar to the ecosystems of network theory, where each collaboration is slightly different from another and, as such, creates its own unique environment (or project ecology). The involvement of the participants, and the arena in which they act, is central to their definition; Bell et al. identify collaborations as 'socially complex organisms, consisting of concrete indi-viduals or groups whose mindsets, dynamics and interests are likely to shape the alliance' (2006:1622).

The aspect of network value and its ability to coordinate across partners for innovation has wider implications. Networks are becoming ever more impor-tant to the ability of companies in the wider socio-economic sense to operate in an increasingly global way (Benkler, 2006; Castells, 2009). Collaborating is a way to operate effectively in industries of increasing complexity and to be adaptive in a constantly changing digital environment. Networks, with their connecting and empowering characteristics, represent systems where knowl-edge and value reside. For an organisation, the ability to encourage network-ing becomes critical in order to develop the more innovative ways of operating that enable entrepreneurial collaborations to work. Any organisation, large or small, will need to recognise how important its network behaviour will be in the future in order to remain competitive and define its value. Businesses like publishing need to be aware of the impact its structure can have on its capacity to operate effectively in a networked economy.

This chapter has focused on the way network theories can be applied to publishing in order to understand ways creative collaborations can form and operate. Networks are an important part of the way a publishing company can respond to its competitive environment. Project-based, collaborative working is becoming more widely used as a way to compete effectively in challeng-ing marketplaces that are undergoing big changes; networks, therefore, are an obvious route to ensure companies connect effectively. Examining the qual-ity of the network involved, and the way it behaves, is one way to test the nature of new digital collaborations. By understanding their processes and their organisational aspects, publishers can exploit these as they develop the sort of innovative projects they may need in the future.

References

Adams, M., Makramalla, M., Miron, W., (2014) Down the rabbit hole: How structural holes in entrepreneurs' social networks impact early venture growth. *Technology Innovation Management Review* 4(9), 19–27. https// doi.org/10.22215/timreview/828

Bell, J., den Ouden, B., Ziggers, G.W., (2006) Dynamics of cooperation: At the brink of irrelevance. *Journal of Management Studies* 43, 1607–1619. https://doi.org/10.1111/j.1467-6486.2006.00653.x

Benkler, Y., (2006) *The Wealth of Networks: How Social Production Transforms Markets and Freedom.* New Haven: Yale University Press.

Bérubé, J., Gauthier, J.-B., (2023) Managing projects in creative industries: A compromise between artistic and project management values. *Creative Industries Journal* 16, 76–95. https://doi.org/10.1080/17510694.2021.197 9278

Bilton, C., (2006) *Management and creativity: From creative industries to creative management.* Chichester: John Wiley & Sons.

Borgatti, S., Lopez-Kidwell, V., (2011) Network theory, in: *The sage handbook of social network analysis.* London: Sage.

Burt, R.S., (2004) Structural holes and good ideas. *American Journal of Sociology* 110, 349–399. https://doi.org/10.1086/421787

Castells, M., (2009) *The rise of the network society: Information age: Economy, society, and culture,* 2nd Edn. Chichester: Wiley-Blackwell.

Collins, R., (1998) *The sociology of philosophies.* Cambridge, MA: Harvard University Press.

Corbett, F., Spinello, E., (2020) Connectivism and leadership: Harnessing a learning theory for the digital age to redefine leadership in the twenty-first century. *Heliyon* 6, e03250. https://doi.org/10.1016/j.heliyon.2020.e03250

Daskalaki, M., (2010) Building 'bonds' and 'bridges': Linking tie evolution and network identity in the creative industries. *Organization Studies* 31, 1649–1666. https://doi.org/10.1177/0170840610380805

Davies, R., Sigthorsson, G., (2013) *Introducing the creative industries: From theory to practice.* London: Sage.

DeFillippi, R., Grabher, G., Jones, C., (2007) Introduction to paradoxes of creativity: Managerial and organizational challenges in the cultural economy. *Journal of Organizational Behavior* 28, 511–521.

Flew, T., (2013) *Global Creative Industries,* Cambridge: Polity.

Grabher, G., (2004a) Learning in projects, remembering in networks? Communality, sociality, and connectivity in project ecologies. *European Urban and Regional Studies* 11, 103–123. https://doi.org/10.1177/0969776404041417

Grabher, G., (2004b) Temporary architectures of learning: Knowledge governance in project ecologies. *Organization Studies* 25, 1491–1514. https:// doi.org/10.1177/0170840604047996

Graham, J., Gandini, A., (2017) Introduction: Collaborative production in the creative industries, in: Graham J., Gandini A. (Eds.), *Collaborative Production in the Creative Industries*. London: Westminster University Press, pp. 1–14. https://doi.org/10.16997/book4.a

Granovetter, M., (1985) Economic action and social structure: The problem of embeddedness. *American Journal of Sociology* 91, 481–510.

Granovetter, M.S., (1973) The strength of weak ties. *American Journal of Sociology* 78, 1360–1380.

Heebels, B., Oedzge, A., van Aalst, I., (2013) Social networks and cultural mediators: The multiplexity of personal ties in publishing. *Industry and Innovation* 20. https://doi.org/10.1080/13662716.2013.856621

Hesmondhalgh, D., (2013) *The cultural industries*, 3rd Edn. London: Sage.

Kung, L., (2008) *Strategic Management in the Media*. London: Sage.

McKinlay, A., Smith, C. (Eds.), (2009) *Creative labour: Working in the creative industries, critical perspectives on work and employment*. Basingstoke: Palgrave Macmillan.

Parker, A., (2004) *Multiplexity*. www.connectedcommons.com/wp-content/uploads/2016/06/Connected-Commons-Multiplexity.pdf

Sawyer, K., (2017) Group Genius: *The Creative Power of Collaboration*. London: Hachette.

Scolari, C., (2019) Networks, in: *The Oxford handbook of publishing*. Oxford: Oxford University Press, pp. 127–146.

Sennett, R., (2012) *Together: The rituals, pleasures and politics of cooperation*. London: Penguin.

Starkey, K., Barnatt, C., Tempest, S., (2000) Beyond networks and hierarchies: Latent organizations in the U.K. television industry. *Organization Science* 11, 299–305.

Thompson, J.B., (2012) *Merchants of culture: The publishing business in the twenty-first century*. Cambridge: Polity.

Uzzi, B., (1997) Social structure and competition in interfirm networks: The paradox of embeddedness. *Administrative Science Quarterly* 42, 35–67.

Uzzi, B., Spiro, J., (2005) Collaboration and creativity: The small world problem. *American Journal of Sociology* 111, 447–504. https://doi.org/10.1086/432782

Wittel, A., (2001) Toward a network sociality. *Theory, Culture & Society* 18, 51–76. https://doi.org/10.1177/026327601018006003

6 Collaboration

Formation, operation and outcomes

Introduction

The next two chapters present the research case studies, using four cases to examine how the theories around collaborations and related network theories explored in the previous chapters play out. This chapter examines how collaborations form and operate, and how participants present the outcomes, looking at the three cases that are project-based. The following chapter looks more closely at organisational behaviour in relation to digital development, examining the wider aspects of networks and the structures that collaborations adopt in relation to the parent companies from which the collaborative partners come.

The project-based cases each take a newly developed product from a different sector. This chapter explores whether the particular characteristics identified in the previous chapters, in relation to the formation, operation or ambition of a collaboration, help ensure success of a project. While it had not been part of the original sampling strategy, it happened that the three product cases achieved financial and critical success: one is still available as an interactive book, and two are being actively developed in a continuous way years on, reflecting the iterative and expansive nature of digital development.

Case studies overview

This chapter presents the three product cases; the fourth case focuses more on organisational behaviours. These product cases are summarised as follows:

Case 1, an example of a *consumer-oriented* game book, examines the way different creative people, from composers to game producers, come together to work on a project and extend it through their collective creativity. The case involves creative individuals rather than companies and, as such, reflects a growing importance of the creative network in order to connect, and reconnect, to such people for each new project. The case also highlights an unusual role for publishers as supporters and investors in projects. This product is sold internationally and won several awards at first launch.

DOI: 10.4324/9781003378211-6

Case 2 examines a carefully managed collaboration between a creative organisation and a publisher to produce an *educational* product. This collaboration can be regarded as more traditional in the way it is organised, but it reflects a new approach to working with a creative partner to develop an innovative publishing project. The connection with the creative industries, through the development of the relationship with an arts organisation, is much more embedded and sustained. This interactive, multimedia book was available predominantly in the United States and the United Kingdom.

Case 3 draws out the key issues of a larger *academic* digital project. Formal project management techniques are in place but informality is also required at points; it shows how companies need to negotiate a balance between these two styles of project management for particular types of non-traditional projects. This is particularly important where the scale of the project could disrupt the day-to-day business of the company. In particular, this case shows that, in certain circumstances, collaborating with another publishing company for digital projects may be essential even if in other arenas they remain competitors. This is sold worldwide.

In all the projects there is an element of hand crafting in building the product (unlike standard ebooks). All three project cases are experimental, and so the outcomes are not necessarily guaranteed; in that sense, they are speculative. The organisations admit that they want to try something innovative and take risks. One of the distinctions of collaborations, as opposed to working in traditional transactional ways with suppliers, is that it can encompass something more exploratory. Wood and Gray make the point that 'collaboration can open new and untested possibilities for action, interaction, and relations, and close off existing, well-known ones' (Wood and Gray, 1991:158). For the collaborations under review, something new is being sought, and new networks are being created. It will be important to see how these 'untested possibilities' lead to something tangible for the participants – and help them become explorative and/or entrepreneurial.

Case 1 – consumer interactive book

Formation – new roles, new networks and flexible visions

This project could not have been undertaken by the publisher alone, though it did utilise their skills in content creation and editing as well as marketing. The technical and creative skills for the project came from the digital developer and other creative people involved, such as the illustrator and composer. The application of game development skills to a book product made it innovative, pushing the boundaries of publishing; this merged product reflects the convergence outlined by Weedon et al. (2014).

Notwithstanding their editorial and marketing activities, the publisher's particular role was focused on financing the project, which led to a different sort of relationship. The publisher reinforced the newness of this relationship, acknowledging that 'almost every partnership is new'. The publisher was not purely an investor, as they were involved in ideation; working with those in the wider creative sector had its benefits, as they noted that

> quite often the publisher and the digital publisher have to work so hard to get anyone to come up with ideas; usually you're the one coming up with ideas so it was nice for somebody to come along with . . . an amazing idea and I was really excited.

Even as an investor, the publisher commented that there was not much pressure on the project to achieve success in financial terms. It reflected therefore the Kaats and Opheij (2014) model for an explorative and experimental collaboration whereby simply being involved in the project is an end in itself: participants do not predict what the end goals are in very specific terms; instead they are open to seeing what emerges from the project (Kaats and Opheij, 2014:25). The participants worked in an entrepreneurial way and were able to spot an opportunity to do something innovative from this partnership.

Networks were crucial in the formation of this product, reflecting the importance of both old and established networks operating like latent organisations (Starkey et al., 2000) as well as new networks that brought in creativity for idea development and problem solving. An example of building the collaboration using an older network can be seen in the relationship between publisher and digital developer which was already well established; initially, the publisher had connected to the developers on a previous digital project where they had brokered a relationship between an author and the developers; this time, with an established relationship, they moved into a more innovative area of storytelling.

Meanwhile, new networks led to the illustrator and composer coming on board, and with them came new ideas (e.g. in how to structure the illustrative elements to be reusable in myriad ways). Both described serendipitous moments that led to their connecting to the project: the composer had been writing speculatively following an alphabetical list of emails, while the illustrator had made a chance connection at an event years previously. They realised they were like minded but didn't have a project at that stage; this reflects an aspect of new network formation that emerges from the theories of Burt (2004) and Granovetter (1973). They both added to the richness of the product with divergent thinking.

It is noteworthy that key players, in what was a very small team, came on board through different routes, reflecting the different ways the network behaved. Grabher (2004) would suggest that open networks are the most appropriate way to form creative projects, ensuring variety and diversity; each of these participants reflect open network behaviour in the way they joined the project.

This project also had a well-articulated vision of the product from the start; yet due to the small size of the team, all participants were able to shape it further in creative ways. For example, the illustrator brought a clear consideration of branding into their work, while the composer combined classical and modern elements, reflecting that at the heart of the project was a classic story. A strong vision was key to its success in terms of everyone being on board and clear about what they were working towards, but by having the flexibility to let it evolve, it became a stronger product.

Operation – small teams and autonomy

This development of the vision reflects the way the project operated going forward. As a small, highly organised, experienced group of people made up the team, the culture of the team was significant in achieving the project outcomes. The working relationships were very strong because of the team size. The publisher commented: 'what you have is a small focused team who are extremely experienced and expert in the area, putting absolutely everything into realising that vision'. It could be detrimental to a project if a freelance creative team is not on board or the developers are too hierarchical and closed to other people's ideas. However, in this case the team was close knit, committed and always listening to each other. It reflects the sort of nimbleness noted by Bilton (2006) and Kung (2008) in terms of ways to instil creativity: the publisher recognised that it worked because 'the kind of people who are closest to the project are in charge and are supermotivated'.

In support of this, the style of management was relatively relaxed, underpinned with a level of trust that the different creative people would get on and do what they needed to do. As such it did not require heavy-handed project management; while it had schedules and deadlines, it combined formal and informal approaches. Autonomy did not mean isolation: being a small consultative group, they could respond quickly to new ideas and make decisions promptly. As the illustrator noted, 'the people you are talking with are the people who have all the decisions, they don't rely on a third person'. This freedom from the main organisation in the case of the publisher meant they could be much more agile. In this way the ecosystem of the project (Grabher, 2004) was such that they could become more hands-on and push the boundaries of their involvement beyond the brief.

Outcomes

Finance and risk

This project was very successful in financial terms as well as in its originality. However, the motivation for many of the partners was more vested in the creativity and challenge of the project than in commercial reward. There was no major expectation of financial rewards; rather, team members were interested in testing whether this sort of digital storytelling could be done – combining gaming elements while maintaining a 'bookness'. This could be seen by the fact that non-gamers enjoyed playing/reading it as noted by the illustrator. Both the illustrator and publisher commented on the reputational value of the project: the publisher commented that their final measure of success was about being seen as a forward-thinking publisher – part of its symbolic value.

While risk was felt to be high in terms of success at the start, in retrospect participants considered that they could have taken much greater risks and achieved more, because innovation requires risk taking. The lack of financial expectations perhaps limited the possibilities as they played safe. The publisher acknowledged that, while in hindsight they would have invested a lot more, that understanding came only with hindsight. This reflects a dilemma for publishing – the financial risks they undertook in this case were still based on traditional publishing approaches to risk, but risk may need to be understood and managed differently for digital innovation.

The unusual role of the publisher as investor was as the publisher noted: 'actually does play to some of the strengths a publisher has so it is definitely worth doing more'. He saw this as a 'broadening of collaborative partners' which could be used for further projects in other ways – acknowledging that every project is different and has to be taken on its own terms.

Creativity and learning

One of the key things about explorative and entrepreneurial collaborations (Kaats and Opheij, 2014) is that often a key outcome for participants is the learning. This was certainly apparent for this case and not just around learning different sorts of development skills. The diversity of the team involved supported problem solving; for instance, the illustrator noted that 'some of the things that were tricky aspirations in terms of usability were finally solved by visual resources'. There was clearly a match between the culture in which the collaboration operated and the keenness of the participants to bring their different skills and experience to the collaboration.

What was significant for the publisher was seeing how innovative the project could be: 'every single aspect of the product is incredibly creative . . . this is saturated with creativity'. They learnt from the digital developers that 'the game audience is much more sophisticated at understanding these new ways of telling stories and engaging with them than a traditional audience'.

Case 2 – educational text

Formation – entrepreneurial collaborations and broker roles

As with the first case, this collaboration appeared to fit the entrepreneurial type of collaboration as laid out by Kaats and Opheij (2014). These can lead to several different outcomes: it 'could be directed at anything: penetrating new markets, developing new products, developing new technologies' (2014:26). The ambition of this collaboration was to do all three in the educational sector: both organisations had intimate knowledge of the sector, but were using technology in a new way for the development of texts. The publisher and the arts organisation recognised they could not do what they wanted to achieve alone, being 'unable to renew on their own strength' (Kaats and Opheij, 2014:26). In this case the collaboration was centred on two organisations rather than on a wider range of partners; these two organisations, however, came from different areas of the creative industries and had not collaborated with anyone from the other's sector before, making this an unusual partnership, and purposefully not a traditional transactional relationship (Kaats and Opheij, 2014). While their home organisations were different creative sectors, there were enough commonalities between them to work effectively; they recognised they were on mutually familiar territory, yet also acknowledged that in order to come together effectively, this collaboration would require new ways of working.

The connection that was made between the arts educationalist and the publisher was facilitated by an arts project manager who had extensive publishing experience and had freelanced in the arts sector for many years. They acted as a broker with a level of social capital that meant they were able to bring together the various participants in the project (including those more widely involved freelancers who came to the project via the publisher).

This broker role exemplifies the centrality of trust in network terms (Borgatti and Lopez-Kidwell, 2011:9; Burt, 2004:388). The relationship between the arts educationalist and the arts project manager was a strong tie. This trust then appeared to spread along the network as the other partners became involved, whose connections reflected looser ties. This concurs with the way entrepreneurial networks operate: loose ties exist between participants, and the broker brings them together through his strong ties with the different participants. It is consistent with network theory and the broker role that he was central to enabling trust to be established between partners. While the broker initially was not a project manager, his centrality to the network meant he became one for the collaboration.

The project manager also acted as a knowledge broker because of their expertise in both creative sectors. This was a unique position, meaning they could share their knowledge between the partners; as they explained, they were able to understand 'both languages' – the requirements of the publisher, and the demands and ethos of the arts organisations. This was recognised as valuable by other participants: as the publisher noted, 'that is where we were very fortunate, they had their foot in both camps'.

The particular benefit for the project was the way the broker person set up and managed the collaboration: this helped the project through a 'process of osmosis' as they developed a formula that worked for both organisations. It was clear, though, that any broker role is only as strong as the engagement from other parties, and so ties in the network need to operate both ways to be fruitful.

This was reflected also in the way the vision was developed and how the participants connected with the vision. While the idea started at the arts organisation end, the arts project manager became the broker of the overarching vision to the publisher and specialist freelancers as they came on board. In this way the publisher and freelancer could be described as vision stakeholders, and they continued to develop the vision; they were therefore, not just following a brief but actively committing into the vision and taking ownership. Both the central and wider teams were very much invested in the project, and, as with the first case, they played a significant role in the vision, acting as stakeholders, under the steering of the project manager: as the freelancer notes, they were 'brilliant and conceiving what this might be and holding together all the different parts of it'. This strength of vision continued through the project.

Operation – autonomy and avoiding disruption

The broker role remained central to the success of the collaboration: it operated smoothly with limited conflict because of that person. They put a relatively formal project management process in place and chaired steering committee meetings; there was a recognition in the partnership that each side had decisions for which they should be properly responsible, but that they would need to bring these to meetings to ensure agreement, keeping the process consultative. Those wider stakeholders in the vision had roles to play and had authority because of their expertise. The trust between partners allowed them to reach compromises over, for instance, marketing language.

Success also seems to have been invested in the fact the participants acted autonomously of their own organisations. Participants were senior in their organisations and mostly, or entirely, given authority by their organisations to take decisions. As the publisher noted, 'we don't need to go through 'x' number of committees to get there', and the arts educationalist said: 'the team has autonomy. I am just one of the team'. The network was strong in enabling decision making to happen swiftly.

The work undertaken by the publisher side of the project was notably more than for the first case. A number of people from the publishing side undertook activities for the project but were not part of the central or the wider team: for example editorial, proof readers, data managers, etc., stayed within their own spheres of working within the publisher. While they had specific roles, autonomy and expertise of their own, they stayed within the functional roles that sat within the publisher's home organisation and did not form part of the core collaborative team. It was less necessary for those working in house to buy into the holistic vision for the product. The project was slotted into the publisher's workflow in standard ways; for instance, when a piece of content needed copy editing, it would be inserted into the standard schedules.

It appeared as if they were running two organisational approaches alongside each other: one being the project specifically and the other the day-to-day workflow for their ongoing publishing activities. As the publisher noted, the project 'went through the standard production run throughs, scheduling monitoring of progress, monitoring of money, all the checks and balances you would apply to a normal textbook project'. In such a way the project was able to sit within the publisher in a 'business as usual' way, while the innovative side of the collaboration sat separately; the complexity of the project did not therefore distort the day-to-day work of the publisher.

Outcomes

Finance and risk

The collaboration resulted in an exceptionally good interactive digital learning product that was very well regarded by the market. While there was a clear vision for what the product would look like, as the project manager articulated, at its heart the result of the collaboration was essentially a new approach to curriculum development; this was not articulated as an expected outcome at the start. As an entrepreneurial collaboration, the expectations of the project were relatively fluid: compromises had to be made with the vision between the two main partners, but the success of the product that emerged was a combination of the two organisations' pedagogic approaches. Financial aspects were a consideration, but so too were the creativity of the project and the value of the partnership that had developed.

However, rather with case 1, while the risk taking felt big at the time and both organisations took a leap of faith in the view of the project manager, in retrospect it might have limited the scope of the project as participants considered that perhaps greater risks should have been taken. While they felt they were at the 'cutting edge' of innovating around a project, participants wondered if some of the compromises they made led to a sense of missed opportunities; for example, more extended market research might have supported further developments in the content around exam material and around sales processes. The collaboration operated so smoothly that it may have missed an opportunity to be more innovative.

Creativity and learning

There was unanimity that the actual digital projects looked very good, fresh and innovative. There were other creative aspects: the project management style for this sort of project was new to both organisations; the contract that was designed for the partners was bespoke; and they developed an approach to curriculum design. The team learnt together how to experiment in a digital environment and to do so without distorting the day-to-day work of either organisation. Designing an approach to experimentation is important: as the publisher said, 'the key is not to disrupt your core business but to use the way the core business works to create the product that comes out of the collaboration'.

Case 3 – academic online resource

Formation – networks and brokers

Unlike the other two cases, this academic project had a clear remit from the start, initiated by the lead publisher, making use of their extensive selection of historical and contemporary texts. As with the previous cases the collaboration is entrepreneurial in the way it operated, in particular because it had to work with competitors. To make it market leading, it needed critical mass; as the digital director said, 'we came to the conclusion that we needed more than our content to be represented in that platform to make it different and distinct'. So they asked competitors to join them in the digital project. Alliances that are entrepreneurial are 'designed to promote invention and development'; in order for companies to develop and renew, they 'need a complementary partner' (Kaats and Opheij, 2014:27) even if, at times, this means companies work with competitors. The publisher noted: 'it's a very unusual relationship as obviously in the print world we compete directly'.

As with case 2, this case had a similar approach to managing the balance between day-to-day activities and the innovation management of the project itself. Roles such as the management of digital rights acquisition and textual editorial work on content were based in house and scheduled into their workflows. The lead publisher, however, also recognised it would need to work with innovators outside their own company, as they did not have the expertise in house. So a separate team was set up to work on developing the project itself, combining in-house and external people.

The publisher made use of networks to identify external collaborators to bring into the project for ideation, design specifications, and software development. It is notable that these collaborators were all people who had worked in publishing before. In the way the broker of case 2 was able to connect two worlds, so these consultants were able to understand both the culture of software development and the culture of the publisher. They could work on the structure of data while also understanding the nature of the content and how it was used by its audience: as one commentator noted, 'One of the things I hope I bring to this kind of project is a mixture of technical know-how and also knowing the content, having an affinity with the content and the context'. Another noted that it meant you could balance innovation with what was achievable: that the aim for the project was to make it 'both as ambitious as it should be and as practical as it needed to be'.

The consultants acted as knowledge brokers who could understand both sides of the picture, particularly as the project was so complex that it could not follow standard development procedures. As the digital publisher noted, 'The economics of these are so content-dependent it raises lots of other perspective and problems'. Understanding the content and the value of it became important.

In terms of their relationship with the competitor publishers, there was a high level of trust; they had to share access to their authors as rights were being collected, for example. The lead publisher kept the others informed, but the relationship between them was 'kind of pretty hands off so that was a good achievement . . . they actually trusted us enough and relied on our expertise in developing these products'. They relinquished some levels of control on the basis of this trust, but structures were put in place to ensure communication was clear and open.

Operation – autonomy and flexible project styles

Overall, the number of people involved at the heart of the project and steering it forward was small, so it could move quite flexibly – reflecting the previous two cases. There was a recognition that this would be a complex and involved project, so people needed to be taken out of their day-to-day jobs to focus on the project at its development stage. As with the other cases, the project team members were senior people who could take decisions, and the project could move forward without distracting anyone else from the ongoing activity of the publisher.

New roles were created specifically for this as the scope of the project emerged. For example, they recruited a digital project manager, as it was clear the content engineer should not also be doing this role. This was a new departure for the publishing house, and the digital manager noted, 'I think that some publishing companies do not price the value of project management when they go into digital'.

Even with this formal project role, there was a recognition that more formal structures can be problematic and hinder fast progress. The publisher, content engineer and digital project manager all agreed that the project was relatively un-hierarchical. While software development processes can follow relatively formal protocols, the digital manager felt that the flexibility of an agile approach allowed the project to change in iterative ways, and it was able to move at relative speed; the team's autonomy facilitated this. There are dangers in this: as the digital consultant noted, some important detail can be lost early if it is not planned out at the start and which then comes to 'bite you'. In this case, it appears a hybrid project management style was adopted which included some formal approaches of traditional software development, combined with flexibility when needed to move quickly.

Outcomes

Finance and risk

The product was a success and continues to be actively developed on an ongoing cycle of continuous iteration. By having all the partners involved, the publisher said, 'it went from being a good project to being a great project'. The consultant felt that there was a market-building aspect to their working together: they 'basically created a market space which epitomised online products'.

As with the other cases, measures of success were varied, as is characteristic of explorative and entrepreneurial collaborative activity. The financial outcome was not the only measure of success for this sort of new product launch; and, as with the second case, the content was of high quality, so the key was to ensure the digital version worked exceptionally well even as a minimum viable product. This was important also for attracting further partners and the longevity of the product: this sustainability was core to the vision from the start.

Creativity and learning

There was creativity in the product itself. For example, external partners considered innovative ways to navigate the content, and several impressive search tools were developed through the collaboration. The publishing company recognised that they learnt a lot about the way projects like this should be structured and how organisations can manage projects effectively going forward. First was an understanding of digital workflows: they recognised 'it was not a giant book' but needed a cultural change to encompass this. The publisher stated that the consultant helped her think differently about data and that felt creative for her; she felt the senior management would need to understand this in order to develop further products.

The digital manager recognised another important aspect of organisational learning: the new roles that emerged through the project needed to be expanded, not just around project management but about managing the growing number of partnerships and relationships that a publisher might need. From this the biggest impact of this project was the plan for the publisher to develop a digital unit in house. The publisher described the cumbersome process of continuing to develop a product with external companies: valuable time could be lost as software developers had their own priorities and own budgets, so they recognised the need to bring the ongoing development of the platform in house. While the creative and innovative part of this project worked most effectively when taken outside of the main business, to sustain the project once up and running would require more in-house expertise and specialisms.

Reviewing the cases

All three cases displayed a combination of entrepreneurial and explorative characteristics (Kaats and Opheij, 2014), representing new sorts of collaborative activity for publishers; they were exploring opportunities to be innovative, with loose goals centred on understanding new markets or product types. Similar themes emerged through the cases at each stage of the collaborative process that reflect these sorts of collaborations.

Formation

Size of the collaboration and vision

The projects all involved small numbers of people. As Leadbeater notes, a small creative network is the one that allows for diverse voices to be heard and flexible working practices to be put in place (2009). All these projects, in their development stages, operated as small satellite groups, separate from the day-to-day business of the publishing company. Small, manageable sizes are important for complex projects; everyone is alert to the central goal and keeps to the core vision (Kaats and Opheij, 2014; Kung, 2008). The small team provides an emotionally supportive environment that allows people freedom to express creative ideas (Farrell, 2003; Levine and Moreland, 2004; Sawyer (2017). A small group is often more effective at reaching creative solutions (Gauntlett, 2011).

One further aspect of the formation stages of collaboration is the importance of the vision development that is both focused and flexible. A characteristic of all three projects is the clarity of their vision. The vision can be clearly articulated between a small group which 'becomes a source of inspiration with a mobilising effect' (Kaats and Opheij, 2014:57). A further aspect of the flexibility of the vision is that it can evolve over time. The people at the core of the project are very close-knit and focused on the vision; this makes it easier for new ideas to come to fruition that can lead to a development of the vision.

The broker and their network

Even a small project team requires some catalyst to draw the team together. It is significant that the three project cases all involve people who played the part of a broker. This role is particularly important at the forming, or convening stage of a collaboration (Farrell, 2003; Levine and Moreland, 2004; Wood and Gray, 1991). These brokers sit in more than one camp, at the heart of an entrepreneurial network, and make connections across structural holes (Burt, 2004; Granovetter, 1973). This, in turn, leads to new opportunities as brokers nurture the knowledge exchange that is required for innovation: 'Idea generation at some point involves someone moving knowledge from this group to that, or combining bits of knowledge across groups' (Burt, 2004:356).

As publishers increasingly look at ways to collaborate beyond the boundaries of their traditional operations, identifying types of people who can become brokers is valuable to cross gaps in any network, make new connections and recognise the way collaboration can lead to creative opportunities and solutions. These sorts of people are 'collaborative leaders' (Kaats and Opheij, 2014, citing Chrislip and Larson, 1994:85); they are people who can 'bring together interested parties, facilitate their interaction, remain neutral, deal with complexity and identify with a range of diverse interests' (Kaats and Opheij, 2014:43); this highlights their interdisciplinarity and their ability to draw together complex innovative collaborations.

Operations

Flexible organisations

Once the projects are formed, their success depends on the ability to set up quickly and for the parent organisations to allow smaller, flexible units to emerge. The different participants are experts in their own area (whether illustrators, software developers, publishers); this expertise allows them all to be able to get on quickly with the project; as such they reflect the characteristic of Starkey et al.'s latent teams (2000).

Kaats and Opheij note that 'cooperation has an intrinsic tendency towards under-organisation' (2014:58), but in the case studies, some formal project management techniques are clearly employed. However, a level of informality is also noted, to allow for creativity and because collaborations are an evolving process (Gajda, 2004). Conditions need to be created to ensure 'effective opportunities for interaction' (Kaats and Opheij, 2014:25) without barriers (Kung, 2008). So stability is required to take risks effectively, but systems must be open enough to encompass new ideas (Uzzi and Spiro, 2005). This balance of formal and informal approaches reflects new styles of working for publishing projects, in contrast with the more formal structures in place centred on traditional workflows.

Decision making and autonomy

A characteristic of all the projects was the level of autonomy vested in the teams. This effectively allowed decision making; it appears that the seniority of people on the central team is a factor. Trust emerging from the network supports this, moving collaborations away from issues of hierarchy and power between partners. These cases reflect Kung's 'small-scale autonomy' (2008:221): that large organisations are flexible and confident enough to allow individuals independence when they operate in creative teams. It suggests that publishers need to allow senior or expert people, with decision-making power, to participate in projects as part of the prerequisite for successful projects of this sort; these are often likely to be the same people developing valuable networks and brokering new ideas.

Outcomes

Levels of success, learning and creativity

All the projects are concerned with creating products of value, but this is measured not only by financial success; the commercial imperative for the product is generally not rated as high as other reasons for undertaking the collaboration: from learning new skills, understanding the innovation process, being creative and exploring new market opportunities. In these cases the collaboration has led to a pioneering development in terms of new digital platforms for content and creative products. The strategic importance of the projects for being forward thinking and innovative is recognised, even where the commercial gain is modest.

The measures of success go wider than the product. In working with a range of new partners there is the expectation among participants that they will learn something new from each other, whether about technology, user experience, readerships or markets. They all have in common an understanding of, and different sorts of expertise with, content: the collaboration leads to ways of using it differently. As one of the participants in the education case said, 'you are all looking for new ways of thinking about something . . . and helping everybody to grow and think of new ways forward'.

Misgivings amongst the participants centre on levels of risk. There are occasions where larger, perhaps risker, creative leaps could have been made. These projects are successful, so it is difficult to draw a conclusion as to whether further creative leaps would have helped bring further success, or that the success achieved was only because of the successful balance managed between the level of risk and creativity. New understandings of risk are required in these contexts.

Conclusion

These three cases illustrate effective ways of collaborating in order to innovate, and they all reflect certain characteristics that help determine success: these centre on people, project definitions and management. However, they also share characteristics on the way they operate in relation to their wider organisations, which will be explored next.

References

Bilton, C., (2006) *Management and Creativity: From Creative Industries to Creative Management*, Chichester: John Wiley & Sons.

Borgatti, S., Lopez-Kidwell, V., (2011) Network theory, in: *The Sage handbook of social network analysis*. London: Sage.

Burt, R.S., (2004) Structural holes and good ideas. *American Journal of Sociology* 110, 349–399. https://doi.org/10.1086/421787

Chrislip, D., Larson, C., (1994) *Collaborative Leadership: How Citizens and Civic Leaders Can Make a Difference.* San Francisco: Jossey-Bass Publishers.

Farrell, M.P., (2003) *Collaborative circles: Friendship dynamics and creative work.* Chicago: University of Chicago Press.

Gajda, R., (2004) Utilizing collaboration theory to evaluate strategic alliances. *American Journal of Evaluation* 25, 65–77. https://doi.org/10.1177/109821400402500105

Gauntlett, D., (2011) *Making is connecting: The social meaning of creativity, from DIY and knitting to YouTube and Web 2.0.* Cambridge: Polity.

Grabher, G., (2004) Learning in projects, remembering in networks? Communality, sociality, and connectivity in project ecologies. *European Urban and Regional Studies* 11, 103–123. https://doi.org/10.1177/0969776404041417

Granovetter, M.S., (1973) The strength of weak ties. *American Journal of Sociology* 78, 1360–1380.

Kaats, E., Opheij, W., (2014) *Creating conditions for promising collaboration: Alliances, networks, chains, strategic partnerships.* New York: Springer.

Kung, L., (2008) *Strategic management in the media.* London: Sage.

Leadbeater, C., (2009) *We-think: Mass innovation, not mass production.* London: Profile Books.

Levine, J.M., Moreland, R.L., (2004) Collaboration: The social context of theory development. *Personality and Social Psychology Review* 8, 164–172. https://doi.org/10.1207/s15327957pspr0802_10

Sawyer, K., (2017) *Group genius: The creative power of collaboration.* London: Hachette.

Starkey, K., Barnatt, C., Tempest, S., (2000) Beyond networks and hierarchies: Latent organizations in the U.K. television industry. *Organization Science* 11, 299–305.

Uzzi, B., Spiro, J., (2005) Collaboration and Creativity: The Small World Problem. *American Journal of Sociology* 111, 447–504. https://doi.org/10.1086/432782

Weedon, A., Miller, D., Franco, C.P., Moorhead, D., Pearce, S., (2014) Crossing media boundaries adaptations and new media forms of the book. *Convergence* 20, 108–124. https://doi.org/10.1177/1354856513515968

Wood, D.J., Gray, B., (1991) Toward a comprehensive theory of collaboration. *Journal of Applied Behavioral Science* 27, 139–162. https://doi.org/10.1177/0021886391272001

7 Collaboration

Structures, networks and ecologies

Introduction

The case study projects share certain characteristics which reflect new ways of collaborating that are entrepreneurial and exploratory rather than functional and transactional (Kaats and Opheij, 2014). The previous chapter showed the way these projects form and operate together, with the outcomes that they look toward, reflecting this more complex form of collaboration. Attributes they all share include the diversity of partners they connect with; the equality of the partners; the focus on being innovative (rather than commercial); and the expectations for the sorts of outcomes that may emerge which centre on learning and creativity. These make them different from traditional relationships and, for these cases in particular, lead to levels of success.

However, to support these sorts of projects effectively, organisations may have to adapt. Having looked at individual projects, this chapter steps back to draw out the themes that relate to the parent companies. At the heart of the challenges around innovation is the fact that each creative collaborative is unique: as Kaats and Opheij suggest, 'most partnerships are actually interim' (2014:27). The projects were all regarded as exciting and effective examples of collaboration by their participants, uniting many diverse elements in one. The freelance project manager of the education case sums up the process: 'it was actually a very integrated project with a number of strands coming together in a glorious way'. But the interviewees also all acknowledged the projects were ambitious and unusual, demanding individualised processes. This makes it more difficult to undertake this type of project development regularly and sits uncomfortably with a traditional print and digital publishing process that is very streamlined. As the publisher in the consumer case noted, it would be a challenge to try to recreate the project as it had 'a very unique set of ingredients to replicate'. The question here is how to align the uniqueness of the projects where innovation is situated with repeatable processes that support ongoing experimentation. Are there organisational, cultural and structural ways publishers can create conditions for these sorts of collaborations?

To explore this, the first part of the chapter continues to examine the three project cases, focusing further on networks and the structural issues parent

DOI: 10.4324/9781003378211-7

companies face in relation to sustaining innovations. The challenges they face, as we have seen, centre on avoiding distorting the day-to-day running of the company while recognising that the innovative project may need to come in house at some point.

There is a further issue: understanding how to stimulate new innovative projects going forward to create a pipeline of innovation. In order to explore this last point, this chapter introduces a fourth case which looked more closely at creating a collaborative culture within an organisation, a culture that sets up conditions for effective collaborations and innovation internally and externally.

This chapter therefore explores how organisational structures can be adapted to allow for certain levels of innovative activity. It concludes with an exploration into the value vested in networks to organisations, and it examines how building collaborative mindsets can support ongoing creative collaborative activity.

Sustaining innovation through collaboration

Organisations need to be innovative and forward facing in order to move as consumers change behaviour and develop new solutions as well as to explore new market opportunities and diverse audiences. Networks and collaborative behaviour are key to this (Castells, 2009). Organisations need to be able to collaborate continuously in order to face the 'complex issues of our day' (Kaats and Opheij, 2014:89) and find sustainable ways to collaborate around new ideas.

There are issues that make it particularly challenging for organisations to undertake this sort of work, as the cases show. It is noticeable that the concepts featured in these projects often take a while to develop. The vision itself takes some time to evolve into something that can become a product idea. The education case, as the most extreme example, took years to become a project; the consumer case would not have come about without the earlier project on which it was built. The processes of getting the academic project underway with specifications and user experience design stages, along with the rendering of content into appropriate formats, meant that it took some time to go live, even as a minimum viable product. New ideas need to be generated, and then ideas need testing out before they can develop into a project. Projects around digital innovation once initiated may take a while to develop.

In a wider sense, it is clear that people within the project cases are outward looking and recognise the need for people to collaborate more; they are the sorts of individuals open to collaboration. However, the manager in the academic case, for example, stated that her team needed help to think about 'how to develop the vision and really think about these sorts of projects, because they are different from book publishing'. Thinking of processes and products that sit outside the norm is more challenging and takes time to embed with teams.

The set-up of the projects is time-consuming. For example, the brokers explored in the previous chapter spent a lot of time getting everyone on board and developing a vision that could be shared with everyone; at the same time they are negotiating between different organisations and the demands of their parent companies. The vision development needs to accommodate the fact that the collaborative partners come from different organisations which have slightly different missions; they may have different expectations as well as different ways of working. The manager at the arts organisation in the education case, when talking about the relationship with the publisher, said 'our missions are different but goals have to be common enough'. The vision has to be flexible to allow for different nuances between organisations, without being dominated by one. The effectiveness of the shared vision is a critical part of a succession collaboration: 'shared ambition has to be one that is important to all the participating organisations' (Kaats and Opheij, 2014:43). This combination of difference and sameness is blended in different ways depending on the project.

Innovation and the day-to-day

These challenges further indicate that keeping the project separate from the main organisations is important. It is a key concern, as already noted, that where the parent organisation is managing an innovation project, with uncertain outcomes, it does not want to distort their ongoing core business.

The three project cases clearly solved this by situating the project outside the mainstream business. Because the innovation process can be long and complex, and levels of risk are unpredictable, a business can hive off failure if necessary while allowing time to work towards success. But it also comes, as outlined, with some pre-requisites to be effective: the project team needs to have devolved power to be able to make decisions, given the new patterns of risk; and so often the make-up is of relatively senior people from the company.

These projects worked as separate, satellite organisations with their own modus operandi. The vision development, as a process of negotiation, took time with all the other project responsibilities, but it was regarded as central to the success of the project and the coming together of the partners. Agreed ways of interacting around decisions were set up at the start as well; this included establishing open forms of communicating as well as the overt application of project management techniques, albeit in a combination of informal and formal types. They all drew on resources of the main organisation in precise ways at specific times and didn't try to flow the whole project into the ongoing systems of the companies involved. In this way they had autonomy to keep moving forward, rather than having to consult back with the parent organisations; yet they were able to draw on key expertise as required. This combined the effectiveness of the various organisations involved, while maintaining the effectiveness of the project.

Sustaining these projects

There is a further aspect to sustainability: if it is to have longevity, the project needs to find a home once it is up and running. Having recognised that these projects need to operate separately to be effective when being developed, they then face a difficulty when they are ready to integrate back into the publisher's organisation. The education and the academic case have both continued after the launch of the initial project; the education case has moved onto further linked projects, while the academic case has continued a rolling programme of development. In these initial collaborations, specific ways of operating are put into place that separate the project from the main publishing house; but over longer terms, it is difficult to maintain a wholly separate way of working. Experimentation can happen separately, but once they are set up, they need more standardised processes to continue. As already noted in the academic case, there were particular requirements to have more control over iterations of the platform, making it an essential stage in its continuing development. In both these cases, the participants suggest that, in the longer term, different approaches need to be taken which they regard as less creative but more sustainable; having purposefully avoided distorting the business, they then need to find a way to fit in after all.

In those cases, the projects remain central to the strategy of the publishing houses; the houses therefore need to design ways to ensure continuing balance between new collaborative creativity and sustainable, integrated business practice. The initial project sponsors are not involved, and the ongoing management of the relationship is handed on to a new staff structure. The participants who had moved on from their projects mentioned that there were now new ways of working in house, including organising around project teams using hybrid project management methods, bringing software development in house and formal scheduling of product iterations; this involved new roles such as content management systems and ongoing roles around relationship building. With the ideation stages over, the projects could be normalised in processes and more effectively integrated into the traditional processes of the publisher. It is the innovative and creative stage that requires separateness and a free reign. But once a structure and process is established, while it may require a different departmental structure, broadly they can fit back with the home organisation.

There is a dilemma here. The organisation needs to maintain some of the style of the original collaboration so as not to lose the qualities of successful collaborative relationships, but it needs to move on and integrate the projects; the senior staff involved in the original project are not necessarily able to continue with the collaboration in an ongoing way (particularly given the level of seniority and experience they may represent). Yet the creative aspects of the collaboration that led to the original innovation may be lost if it is integrated too far into the core of the business. In addition, to continue to develop innovative projects, the organisation needs to be able to move onto the next new partnership and maintain an ability to enter into new creative projects, using the staff who are experienced at collaborative work in this way.

Therefore, creating an effective environment in which to collaborate in an ongoing way is also important. This means a more lasting collaborative environment needs to be created as the project continues. The participants in these cases all recognised the need to collaborate over a period of time, with changing personnel and evolving project visions. The academic team saw limits in using a lot of external people to collaborate; at each stage it is time consuming, while nimbleness and cost-effectiveness is better achieved with some more in-house expertise. Their solution was to bring many of the aspects of the original project into their organisation; ongoing agility comes to be achieved more effectively with more in-house development, though there will remain a question about how innovative it can continue to be if in-house processes begin to take over. There remains, then, a question about sustaining the creativity of projects even when they come in-house.

Organisational case study

Developing a culture for ongoing collaboration is important on two counts – both for the innovative work in the first place, and for maintaining a level of agility and creativity once a project returns to the main organisation. If each project is unique, then finding new partners and developing new ideas is key for developing a pipeline of innovative projects.

As the projects show, the network is critical. Networks need to bring connections with a wider, more diverse set of people, often from other creative industries, but which bring enough divergent thinking to look at markets in different ways and consider solutions. Also key is the role of the broker, who may not be the most creative person in the team, but is the person who can make connections, draw in new people and spot opportunities. To do this, brokers build entrepreneurial networks; recognising that not all ideas will come to fruition; seniority plays a part here too, as brokers can spot opportunities and have a level of autonomy to make forays into new areas. However, there need to be conditions for people to be open to developing networks or become brokers. The fourth case looks at how a culture of openness may help lead to the serendipitous collaborations that become innovations.

This case was based at a global STM publisher and looked at the elements of a change programme, with structures and workspaces that were explicitly related to the desire to encourage more collaborative activity in the company. The case explores the ways that external and internal collaborations can be encouraged through organisational culture, communication and workplace environments, recognising that people need to be open to collaboration in order to learn and develop new projects and improve processes.

The company was concerned to support cross-fertilisation of ideas through establishing a culture of collaboration. This was done in a variety of ways. A new workspace design was built, with pods, hubs and open collaborative spaces including social areas, to encourage easy mixing between different departments as well as provide flexible spaces to support the ability to have informal impromptu meetings in person and online. The organisation also established an intranet which focused on making it easy to find out about and connect with others across the organisation globally. A variety of regular cross-departmental activities was designed to encourage learning across the organisation as well as communications around the importance of creativity and interconnectedness. The research focused on conversations with individuals regarding how they had found these aspects of the change programme and was designed to explore levels of awareness around collaboration. The organisation's aim was to help individuals develop collaborative ways of thinking, which in turn would help create the collaborative organisation (Sawyer, 2017). These initiatives were seen by the managers to offer the opportunity for the company to adapt to a changing environment.

The research showed that across participants at different levels and in different departments, all had engaged with the themes of the change and were talking about the cultural change towards a more collaborative environment, embodied by the workspaces and the intra-departmental communications. Part of what the staff felt was effective was the flexibility to work in the way you wanted and to feel that if you had an idea, it could be heard due to the emerging level of openness across the organisation. The collaborative environment enabled product ideas to evolve, and participants noted how easy it was to moot an idea or pilot something in the organisation.

Participants acknowledged that the communication around collaboration was explicit: this was the overarching theme to the changes at the organisation, and so everyone was highly aware of it, but they felt, and even valued, the benefits. For the people interviewed, the importance of collaboration was about needing to innovate and be constantly changing as a response to the world around them. As the journals manager noted, 'change leads to an absolute need for collaboration'. The production manager reflected that this led to a need to nurture certain types of people:

> people that listen and seek information from other people will be the ones who keep moving forward and the ones who sit in their silos will not be able to do quite as much, or be able to innovate quite as much, to reach the same kinds of solutions.

Therefore, collaboration was not just about connectedness but also about thinking 'out of the box' and becoming more creative about possibilities and problem solving.

In the programme there was a focus on developing a mindset amongst staff, where employees would feel empowered and move out of functional areas, to the point of rethinking approaches to product development. This case showed how to get everyone in the organisation to understand the importance of collaboration and break out of the sort of traditional mindsets that the academic manager in the project case felt was apparent and which could limit ideas. This was summarised in this case by the production head, saying:

I have seen a change in the ethos from very siloed development of new products to a much more collaborative way of working, so a new idea or concept is brought to the table you immediately see different groups fall into [thinking about] that. I think that is probably because the business is moving away from publishing content, in a standard way, to having to present that content differently, more technology focused, so the pool of expertise needed is widening I think'.

Instilling an understanding that collaboration is a way ahead is what the final case appears to have done successfully; everyone interviewed recognised both that collaboration is important and that the corporation is very much focused on developing that culture. The culture that was nurtured in the organisation focused on simplifying the way people connected with each other, through physical and digital spaces.

This STM case also reflects the importance of creating opportunity. It purposefully attempts to set up environments where connections between people might spark off ideas. New ideas can be about new products, but they also see it as an important way to solve problems around increasing efficiency. This case recognises that collaboration and networking will lead to further creativity and knowledge sharing. The collaborative environment that is produced facilitates the opportunity to stimulate more open-ended, experimental collaboration; the aim is to create a culture where exploration can take place. As Kaats and Opheij state, explorative collaborations 'put accessibility and interaction centre stage' (2014:26).

Challenges with collaborative environments

While it is apparent from the fourth case that the environment can help create a collaborative frame of mind, it must be managed appropriately and supported by the behaviour and structure of the organisation. The illustrator in the consumer case cautioned that 'ping pong tables do not solve everything', as he has experienced creative environments where this kind of resource is brought in to try to encourage collaboration. He notes that, coming into publishing from the outside, he had seen publishers try to emulate creative incubator sharing spaces simply to be disruptive. But it can be difficult to do properly: 'it doesn't matter how many things you put there to create that kind of cool, relaxed ambience, you keep the hierarchy the same and people feel intimidated to give an opinion to a manager'. In other words, while an organisation can create an interesting workspace, staff also need to feel encouraged to put new ideas forward, through an open and facilitating, non-hierarchical corporate culture. While structurally only limited changes had been made in terms of the overall management hierarchy, in the fourth case, staff did feel empowered to share ideas and collaborate effectively.

Flexibility of the organisation

Drawing on the research from all the cases, the final part of the chapter explores the characteristics of an organisation that can collaborate effectively: it is one that can create flexible environments, recognises the value of networks and supports conditions for creative project ecologies.

Agility and flexibility are important for responding effectively to change. Developing flexible mindsets that can take up serendipitous opportunities quickly emerged as key in the research across the cases. This is not just about people within projects, but about the flexibility of the wider organisation. The aim of the change programme in the STM case was to facilitate the coming together of teams so that they can configure and reconfigure easily (Bilton, 2006). The variety of connections the space allows, facilitating as it does people mixing up quickly and easily, can lead to new projects. The intranet also leads to people making links to new internal collaborators. In this way the whole organisation works as a network from which new ideas and connections can arise. The organisation allows for the possibility for latent organisations, focused on specific projects, to emerge from the day-to-day business activity; and the workspaces allow collaborations to surface quickly. This allows the organisation to respond quickly to new ideas. This 'flexible, matrix-based' (Bilton, 2006:49) organisation means projects can be assembled quickly, and this embeds a level of organisational creativity in the structure.

Being able to operate flexibly appears, therefore, important for the operation of collaboration. Both the project cases and the workplace case suggest that structural elements can be put in place to facilitate collaboration, whether by allowing projects to emerge and exist alongside the main organisations (as flexible latent organisations) or by making an environment and mindset that encourages nimbleness and connectivity. Both involve a level of flexibility that builds on the concepts of the agile organisations required to face digital transformation effectively (Bilton, 2006; Flew, 2013).

The centrality of networks

While the broker plays a particular role in crossing gaps in networks, the research has shown how the network as a whole is important for effective project formation. If creative collaborations require divergent thinking (Levine and Moreland, 2004), then the quality of the network is important to connect diverse people.

As we have seen in the previous chapter, a blend of older, embedded networks with newly growing entrepreneurial networks appear at play with the project cases. The importance of networks is not only associated with the projects specifically. The loose ties are also reflected in the way people connect before there are any actual projects in development. Chance connections, whereby trust is acknowledged between partners but which may only later bear fruit, reflect the development of a network that may lead to something only in the longer term; therefore, it holds latent value (Wittel, 2001) that emerges when required. The loose ties make it more entrepreneurial (Burt, 2004) so creating an environment where more innovative projects may emerge from divergent groups of people. This could be seen to reflect the outer edges of the publisher's network behaviour examined by Heebels et al. (2013). The knowledge and expertise distributed throughout the network are key here, in order to make decisions quickly and deal effectively with the complexity of the project once it is up and running; this too helps builds the trust between partners which, we have seen, is vital to effective collaborations. The network therefore leads to creativity and diversity but also provides security for effective cooperation (Daskalaki, 2010). The network is of value for being able to lead to innovative responses when activated.

In order to achieve this type of network, the right sort of people are required: they need to have an entrepreneurial outlook in order to straddle the weak ties, make diverse connections and spot opportunities for new projects (Granovetter, 1973). The fourth case reflects a recognition that, through creative and collaborative environments, people like this can be nurtured. In this case the workspace itself opens up opportunities for people to make serendipitous connections, and it facilitates the creation of new links and ties through which knowledge and ideas can flow; in this way, the publisher can encourage new networks to evolve.

Creative project ecologies

As the projects evolve, they develop their own ways of working, their individual project ecologies (Grabher, 2004). The ecologies exhibited in the cases, although different from each other, allow them to utilise creative thinking and problem solving, as well as develop their own approaches to project management and decision making. The projects do not replicate systems, but each project has a different unique approach which in itself can prompt creativity (Grabher, 2004). What is important is recognising that the projects have their own ecology even within the wider ecosystem of the publishing house.

The clearest example of this is the consumer case, where the individuals come together to solve problems and ensure the digital product they produce pushes boundaries and is creative; this is possible due to their very open approach to communication. While there are examples of creative thinking in the education and academic projects, encouraged by the openness of the project ecology, it appears that the most creative project, the gamebook, was the most open to everyone's ideas. This case is the smallest group, but it was formed from the widest range of partners. The participants were also more accustomed to a different creative working culture from the game and advertising sectors. For Grabher, this case would reflect a very creative project ecology (2004); it also reflects how far the participants allow divergent thinking to add to the creativity of the project (Uzzi and Spiro, 2005).

Creative project ecologies provide a system, or social process, for problem solving and cooperating; this means that while the collaboration can be creative and can combine divergent and convergent thinking, by having some sort of structure and a set of implicit rules for decision making, it is managing risk. Here too, the theme of balance emerges as an ecology creates an equilibrium between creative freedom and project structure to ensure things can get done. The ecology itself allows the projects to take risks as it innovates, thus separating out these more unpredictable levels of risk from the main businesses.

Conclusion

The last case reflects a way to tackle the ongoing need to collaborate. The organisation recognises that collaboration can lead to suggestions for improvements and refinements of daily activity, as well as for development of new ideas. By creating an environment that encourages collaborative thinking, they hope to integrate the benefits of collaboration into the business in an ongoing way. Through this, an organisation can create the conditions to stimulate successful new collaborations.

So, where organisations can be flexible, stimulate the development of networks and support creative approaches to project development through creative project ecologies, it can develop a sustained and manageable approach to innovation.

References

Bilton, C., (2006). *Management and creativity: From creative industries to creative management*. London: John Wiley & Sons.

Burt, R.S., (2004) Structural holes and good ideas. *American Journal of Sociology* 110, 349–399. https://doi.org/10.1086/421787

Castells, M., (2009) *The rise of the network society: Information age: Economy, society, and culture*, 2nd Edn. Chichester: Wiley-Blackwell.

Daskalaki, M., (2010) Building 'bonds' and 'bridges': Linking tie evolution and network identity in the creative industries. *Organization Studies* 31, 1649–1666. https://doi.org/10.1177/0170840610380805

Flew, T., (2013) *Global creative industries*. Cambridge: Polity.

Grabher, G., (2004) Learning in projects, remembering in networks? Communality, sociality, and connectivity in project ecologies. *European Urban and Regional Studies* 11, 103–123. https://doi.org/10.1177/0969776404041417

Granovetter, M.S., (1973) The strength of weak ties. *American Journal of Sociology* 78, 1360–1380.

Heebels, B., Oedzge, A., van Aalst, I., (2013). Social networks and cultural mediators: The multiplexity of personal ties in publishing. *Industry and Innovation* 20. https://doi.org/10.1080/13662716.2013.856621

Kaats, E., Opheij, W., (2014) *Creating conditions for promising collaboration: Alliances, networks, chains, strategic partnerships.* New York: Springer.

Levine, J.M., Moreland, R.L., (2004) Collaboration: The social context of theory development. *Personality and Social Psychology Review* 8, 164–172. https://doi.org/10.1207/s15327957pspr0802_10

Sawyer, K., (2017) *Group genius: The creative power of collaboration.* London: Hachette.

Uzzi, B., Spiro, J., (2005) Collaboration and creativity: The small world problem. *American Journal of Sociology* 111, 447–504. https://doi.org/10.1086/432782

Wittel, A., (2001) Toward a network sociality. *Theory, Culture & Society* 18, 51–76. https://doi.org/10.1177/026327601018006003

8 Conclusion

Para-organisations and collaborative mindsets

Introduction

These four publishing case studies lead to an understanding of the nature of creative collaborations and what makes them work most effectively. It is challenging to innovate given the traditional approaches to new product development in terms of risk management, and given that workflows are embedded in the way the industry does things (Hall, 2019, 2022). These standardised processes remain very successful, though they limit certain types of innovation. Yet digital transformation requires some changes in behaviour for the publishing sector.

It is clear from examining the evolution of the publishing industry that it has been continuously innovative both in content (i.e., different types of content for different markets, new ways of writing) and form (from new printing techniques to new formats like Penguin paperbacks). However, though the industry is always evolving, certain aspects of publishing such as the workflow, from manuscript to bookshop, have become central to the way the publishing houses operate. As Murray and Squires say, 'The publishing value chain has remained relatively consistent since the invention of the printing press' (2013:1). This, to some extent, limits certain sorts of digital innovation that would not be able to make effective use of that workflow.

Just as the industry shares characteristics and behaviours with the wider creative sector, it also encounters similar issues and, by connecting more closely with other creative industries, can collaborate to find solutions. In reviewing the arena of both collaboration and network theories in relation to creativity and learning, these publishing collaborations can help illustrate ways to manage new styles of product development for publishing as well as the value in connecting with the wider sector.

The digital challenge

Publishing theorists like Bhaskar (2013) and O'Leary (2011) call for new ways of thinking about publishing in relation to the challenges of the digital environment. Digital transformation has created instability and disruption,

DOI: 10.4324/9781003378211-8

which means that organisations require more creativity and innovation (Kung, 2016). Digital media offers the opportunity to develop new products, but this can be a challenge if a business is not set up to innovate effectively. While publishing innovates and has developed flexible processes in order to do so, digital experimentation is demanding and requires an iterative approach; it needs a different application of resources (e.g. user experience design up front, or rendering of content into adaptable digital formats) and ongoing testing and development, which can be expensive and time-consuming in comparison to the smooth operation of the existing business processes. As noted by Thompson, innovative products need to be led by the market rather than by the technology, so understanding the context of their use is important (2005). Digital products (beyond standard ebooks) tend to be complex and the markets for them can be unpredictable, so publishers can find it challenging to work on them. They may not necessarily have the expertise in house or the money or resources to spend on buying those skills; they may not want to commit to large digital developments when it is difficult to assess the market potential for those sorts of innovations.

The opportunities for creative collaboration

With that context in mind, the project case studies in this research examine the opportunities to innovate through collaboration. The products are all experimental in different ways: the first around game books; the second around an interactive approach to education curriculum; while the third brings together a complex range of different content types working with competitors to develop a product with critical mass. Converged products like these are emerging as part of the new digital landscape; they combine different media (such as audio and video) and combine skills from different sorts of creative businesses (such as game producers, use designers, game illustrators, storyboard writers and music composers) in order to develop new product types. In this way, these projects represent the sort of product diversity that creative businesses need to nurture.

These sorts of projects are possible only where they are able to bring in expertise from other areas and sectors. Collaborating in new ways around digital products is one way to develop expertise and learn from others; collaborations can bring knowledge from others to the project, such as technical capabilities or market understanding; it can also mean that access to different sorts of content and financial risk can be shared between partners where projects are complex and outcomes uncertain. Collaborations can be effective sites for experimentation without disturbing the day-to-day work of the organisation which is operating successfully. As evidenced in the survey, the industry leaders recognise that the structure of their companies may need to be adjusted in order to accommodate new approaches to digital publishing, including the ability to collaborate with a wider range of partners and to do so more frequently.

New-style collaborations

These projects reflect new styles of collaborating. They are entrepreneurial and explorative, suited to the requirements of publishers looking to develop new ways to experiment, develop creative ideas and make connections with new partners. They share important characteristics around the way they behave that suggest successful creative collaborations are ones which are small, flexible and open to different outcomes; participants share knowledge and inspire each other through divergent thinking; the projects reflect the importance of certain types of networks and brokers in their formation; and they require a balance between formal and informal ways of working as well as creativity and risk.

In addition, the projects operate autonomously as they sit outside the day-to-day business, so they do not impact on the existing hierarchies of the businesses and disrupt the main revenue-generating activity of the publisher. The final case provides an example of a way to instil a culture that encourages agility and openness to connect and collaborate in a sustainable way. It is important to create an environment that facilitates network development which can, in turn, lead to further new ideas and collaborations.

Characteristics of collaborations

These characteristics appear essential to the effectiveness of the creative digital collaboration. They can be summarised as follows:

- Networks: entrepreneurial-styled networks are central to their formation, where the structure of the network is loose and allows for creative leaps to be made between new partners, so creating conditions for creative projects.
- Brokers: a broker is commonly needed to spot opportunities, make connections, bring the project members together, formulate the project and keep it on track.
- Vision: the vision of the collaboration needs to be clear, but does not need to be shared very widely in the initial stages.
- Range of partners: the project team needs to include a range of different partners, people who are reasonably senior and who feel empowered to engage with the sort of creative problem solving demanded by digital projects, though with project teams kept reasonably small.
- Autonomy: the project team needs autonomy with regard to making decisions and to sit outside the usual hierarchy of the businesses from which they emerge, so as to be responsive to the project needs rather than tied to the day-to-day operation of the publisher; the level of seniority and expertise of the partners in therefore important.
- Project management styles: the project team needs to balance formal and informal styles of working in their project ecosystem.

- Types of outcomes: the collaboration is expected to lead to a variety of outcomes that reflect not only commercial imperatives but also a recognition of the importance of learning and creativity.

If the shared characteristics of these projects are indicators for success, then the organisation is in a position to manage ways to encourage further innovation. The organisation needs to be flexible to set up innovation projects and learn from them; it needs to be able to nurture brokers inside and outside of the company; and it needs to recognise the value of a network to operate in a new way with new types of project ecologies. Traditional structures in publishing may not be able to accommodate this activity as easily as it should. Kung states, 'organisational structures must move from stable to fluid ones' (2016:193). Organisations, therefore, need processes which support specific projects and which encourage new collaborative activity across the business.

Structural approaches to collaboration

The findings show how collaborations can be set up and managed to achieve innovative outcomes. How can publishers make structural responses to ensure these sorts of effective collaborations continue to take place? From the understanding of network behaviour and creative digital collaboration, two summary concepts can be seen to emerge from the research, concepts which bring to the fore the importance of organisational structure in collaborative activity: *para-organisations* and *collaborative mindsets*.

- *Para-organisations:* where publishing companies can develop an organisational approach for effective digital innovation through smaller collaborative entities
- *Collaborative mindset:* where publishing companies can embed a spirit of collaboration in their corporate culture

These are terms coined by the researcher and emerge from the research, though they require further testing in order to be validated. Building on the publishing cases, the concepts reflect ways in which publishers can think flexibly about their structure and workplace behaviour.

Para-organisation

The first concept focuses on process. The collaborations shown in the cases all sit outside the core business. As such they seem to exist as separate entities alongside the business. The para-organisation is a way of articulating this: it is a small, flexible, alternative organisation which can swiftly step outside of the usual activity of the publisher, sit alongside it and focus on the specific innovation they want to develop. The attributes noted earlier, that are required for ideal collaborations, are then embedded in these organisations.

The product case studies all indicate that a smaller collaborative organisation emerges from the main organisations and exists for the duration of the project. Even where the project is going to continue and evolve, as in the case of the academic product, in its first defining stage people work separately on it until it is up and running. This means that people in the wider organisation are not specifically drawn into the project, even when they may undertake some work on it (e.g. copy editing); rather, the work is fielded to them at the point of need. This means that the standard publishing work needed for the project is undertaken in the usual way when required, while the creative and innovative parts, as well as vision creation and development, are addressed within the project team in their separate entity, orbiting the main organisation like a satellite.

In this way, a para-organisation allows the main organisation to accommodate very different projects that have different requirements (as exemplified by the varied case studies), without the need to set up a specific development arm or to build formal procedures into the existing workflow. Developing a standardised process within an organisation for digital innovation is difficult; each new project is unique. But building an organisational capacity to develop concepts, and a systematic way to deal with such projects when they arise, may be possible.

Additionally, all the projects studied, because they are innovative, are seen to carry some risk; this sort of unpredictable level of risk can then be managed separately from the business through this separate, but linked, structure.

For this sort of satellite organisation to operate successfully, it is important to be able to deploy people effectively, leading to the implication that they are often expert, autonomous and senior people, characteristics previously noted. This requires some organisational consideration on the part of the publisher; they need a structure that is flexible when setting up projects. It also indicates that the organisation needs to be able to nurture the sorts of people that can be part of these para-organisational teams and act as brokers to connect to the wider creative sector.

Collaborative mindset

The second concept focuses on people. The publisher needs to nurture the sort of people that can form collaborations effectively. The final case created an environment where everyone was alert to the possibilities of collaboration. While there is no suggestion that people would not have collaborated before, there was a greater awareness of the opportunities collaboration brings, which the researcher terms *the collaborative mindset*: a collaborative culture is created where people are open to connecting in all sorts of ways and can conceptualise ideas and work effectively with partners – recognising the possibilities around learning and creativity that exist in such connections. This enables the sort of network behaviour that characterises entrepreneurial and creative activity.

It is important to recognise that collaboration is not just about developing innovative new products but, as in the fourth case, leads to iteration for existing products, solving problems or adding improvements to existing workflows. In this way everyone has the opportunity to be collaborative internally as well as externally. A collaborative mindset can be found in an organisation that nurtures people who are open-minded, who are non-hierarchical, who trust each other, who are creative, listen well, share learning and are ambitious about ideas. The characteristics that feature in successful collaborations also needs to exist across an organisational culture. Critically, a collaboration is a conduit for organisational learning, and the ability to learn is embedded in the collaborative process.

Developing creative collaboration and network theories

It is worth noting that these case studies also develop aspects of collaboration and network theories in relation to creative projects. Creative collaborations are frequently entrepreneurial and exploratory together; they provide ways for creative organisations to respond to digital change. While they are often studied in terms of the way they behave in themselves, it is clear from the research that the parent organisation also plays a part in setting up the conditions for effective collaboration, creating an environment that facilitates them. Collaborative cultures can lead to more innovation, and so latent value is vested in the potential of an organisation to develop collaborations. Because of this, increasing collaborative activity can be a defined strategy for an organisation.

Organisations can also do this through developing a certain type of networked behaviour. Networks are dynamic, continuous and most effective for creative collaboration and innovation, where they achieve a balance between strong and weak ties. An organisation can facilitate network behaviour through corporate culture and workspace planning. A network's value lies in its potential for increased creativity and effective experimentation, and it can therefore be seen as an attribute of any organisation seeking to be innovative.

Publishing structures and multidisciplinary approaches

This research also reflects on wider aspects of publishing as a field of study. The structural and organisational concepts of publishing theory tend to focus on the value chain and on the functions, hierarchies and the different sort of capital found in publishing systems. Publishing has evolved around these traditional forms of business structure, streamlining workflow effectively to focus broadly on producing books/ebooks and journals/ejournals. This structure. however, can act as a restraint on other types of activity and requires some re-evaluation. Where product and format diversity are required (in order to build new markets and attract new types of readers), the fixed nature of the traditional structure and hierarchy appears less effective. While there is some expectation that structural models like these are adaptable, nevertheless they may not be as responsive as they need to be to face more complex digital challenges. What this research shows is that other forms of organisational structure are required to support new types of product development within publishing. Instead of the siloes and functional approach embedded in traditional publishing organisations, flexible, adaptive structures are required, whether enabling para-organisations or supporting collaborative cultures.

Furthermore, publishing theory reflects on the systems for managing risk and profit (including definitions of 'value') that are associated with the current value chain. As the research shows, creative collaborations have to exist outside these constraints to be effective; but innovation also needs to be facilitated and sustained, leading to a recognition that the traditional structure is not suited to the sort of creative approaches the publishing industry needs to embrace; concepts of publishing need to move on from traditional systems.

The research also reveals nervousness around disruption of traditional business lines. Publishing has an embedded approach to risk. New risks require new approaches, and introducing more product diversity is challenging. Here too the traditional structure of publishing is potentially limiting its opportunities to innovate and undertake different types of risks. The research suggests that traditional systems of publishing need to be reconsidered in order for the effective development of new business models and innovative products that encourage new audiences and lead to diversity; this is reflected in the microcosms of the collaborations themselves which, within their para-organisations, adopt more flexible and creative approaches to development processes and expected outcomes; through this they become important sites of organisational learning.

In relation to this, there is an additional aspect: in creating collaborative mindsets within an organisation, it reflects the people that make up publishing remain at the heart of its creative activity. A publishing structure needs to accommodate and nurture people to recognise the value vested in them and their networks; this combines both symbolic capital and human capital but goes further, beyond the traditional networks of, for example, agents and suppliers, to reflect connectivity with the wider creative sector. This requires more focus on people in-house, recognising the value of diverse workforces and the importance of building longer-term relationships and sustainable networks.

This research therefore furthers the discourse around value chains and risk as well as creative labour. Publishing theory in terms of structures needs to move beyond the confines of the traditional value chain and hierarchies, what might be regarded as closed systems, and accommodate a focus on more adaptive, flexible organisations that are capable of agile approaches to innovation and risk taking, while nurturing a creative and collaborative workforce.

As with the collaborative teams in the study, different perspectives can bring a richness to the research. Looking at concepts through a variety of lenses drawn from different disciplines can provide depth leading to insights that might be missed otherwise, particularly when dealing with complexity. Bringing aspects of theory from organisational studies and exploring concepts drawn from creativity management theory, for instance, has helped this research reach conclusions on business structures, organisational culture and effectiveness of collaborative activity as applied to the field of publishing. It has helped throw light on the limitations of the traditional publishing structure. In methodological terms, multidisciplinary research also brings a level of rigour: methodologies can be tested, validated and reflected upon to ensure results stand up to scrutiny. The multidisciplinary nature of this study has helped open up thinking and draw out emergent concepts as well as set up clear links to other disciplines such as management theory.

Applications for publishers – the adaptive organisation

As the survey showed, industry leaders are concerned with collaboration as a response to digital change; this research suggests publishers can look at the ways they can support collaborative activity effectively, recognising that certain collaborative characteristics can lead to successful digital product development. Developing collaborative opportunity and encouraging people to develop wider networks are ways they can develop their collaborative activity further. While some publishers do this already, with individuals tasked with looking out for new ideas, it may be valuable to consider developing staff more widely to have collaborative mindsets. Then, once ideas start to come to fruition, adopting strategies that establish the conditions for successful creative collaborations will be important.

With the concepts of the para-organisation and the collaborative mindset, publishing companies do not necessarily need to change their structure radically to accommodate new ways of collaborating. With an understanding of the way collaborations operate and the ability to form smaller project organisations, publishers may be able to accommodate complex digital innovation without major reorganisation. If they develop a collaborative mindset within the company and facilitate collaborative behaviour, they can create a culture whereby new ideas and connections can happen that lead to more organic innovation; this also does not necessarily require radical structural change. By understanding ways to bring experimental projects about and by recognising the sorts of relationships publishers need with the wider creative sector, the creativity and learning that such projects engender can be encouraged. This indicates that publishers need to have an adaptive organisation, whereby a structural readiness allows them to facilitate collaborative behaviour and then to accommodate new-style collaborations when they emerge.

Concluding thoughts

Publishers recognise the importance of innovating across different platforms, including print, audio and digital. However, the increasingly rapid changes of the digital environment bring particular challenges. Continuous innovation around digital formats are required; otherwise, the industry will be overtaken by competitors from other sectors. App developers such as Touchpress and Inkle books now undertake much of their innovative activity without publisher involvement, while technology companies such as Google and Apple see content as a way to drive activity on their platforms and devices. As Bhaskar and Phillips note, 'it would foolish not to anticipate further dramatic ruptures and shifts in the landscape of publishing' (Bhaskar and Phillips, 2019:425).

Given the imperative to change, the question is how far existing publishing structures are able to manage this complexity. Publishing theory, when exploring structures and organisations, focuses on reviewing the value chain, and related models around managing risk, in order to understand publishing systems. These traditional models, while they have been effective in the past, require deconstructing to build more adaptive flexible organisations that can further publishing innovation and respond to the challenges of diversity.

Publishers have a exhibited a level of resilience over the centuries, open to change and adapting to new opportunities. They recognise the need to develop new ways of working in order to compete and grow in a rapidly changing environment; they recognise the importance being a learning organisation with collaborations as centres of that learning; they are collaborating more widely with different sorts of institutions and they are looking at redesigning their organisations to facilitate this. This research shows that if collaborative activity is undertaken in certain ways, then innovative projects will have a greater chance of success. The concept of the para-organisation allows for ways to develop specific projects, while the collaborative mindset required for these projects can be nurtured through workplace culture.

Publishers may need to think about their role differently (as with game book case study) or look at collaborating with competitors (as with the academic case) in order to set up successful digital collaborations. One of the bigger challenges for publishers is not to disrupt their current business activity, which they undertake very successfully, as they experiment with new forms. Complexity around innovation often hinders the ability of the parent company to run creative digital projects easily. However, a more systematic and proactive approach could potentially reap benefits. This research shows that structures can be put in place that allow innovative projects to be set up and managed effectively. It provides evidence that flexible organisational structures can be a way to accommodate and facilitate collaborative activity. Being a nimble and networked organisation is a way to achieve this, as noted by Castells: 'The ability to reconfigure [will be] a decisive feature in a society characterised by constant change and organisational fluidity' (2009:71). The important aspect for publishing organisations is to continue to be flexible, through para-organisation and collaborative mindsets, so they can change and adapt as new challenges arise.

References

Bhaskar, M., (2013) *The content machine: Towards a theory of publishing from the printing press to the digital network*. London: Anthem Press.

Bhaskar, M., Phillips, A., (2019) The future of publishing: Eight thought experiments, in: *The Oxford handbook of publishing*. Oxford: Oxford University Press.

Castells, M., (2009) *The rise of the network society: Information age: Economy, society, and culture*, 2nd Edn. Chichester: Wiley-Blackwell.

Hall, F., (2019) Organisational structures in publishing, in: *The Oxford handbook of publishing*. Oxford: Oxford University Press.

Hall, F., (2022) *The business of digital publishing: An introduction to the digital book and journal industries*, 2nd Edn. Abingdon: Routledge.

Kung, L., (2016). *Strategic management in the media: Theory to practice*, 2nd Edn. London: Sage.

Murray, P.R., Squires, C., (2013) The digital publishing communications circuit. *Book 2.0* 3, 3–23. https://doi.org/10.1386/btwo.3.1.3_1

O'Leary, B.F., (2011) Context first: A unified field theory of publishing. *Publishing Research Quarterly* 27, 211–219. https://doi.org/10.1007/s12109-011-9221-8

Thompson, J.B., (2005) *Books in the digital age: The transformation of academic and higher education publishing in Britain and the United States*. Cambridge: Polity Press.

Index